Prose Prayer & Poetry

Sequel to Ramblings & Rhyme

By Kay Brothers

Copyright ©Kay Brothers

All rights reserved

ISBN 978-0-6488216-0-1
First Edition 2022
Photos from Family collection
Illustrations – Mika Miyake
Editor and publisher Dana McCown

StoryBridge Press

Brisbane, Queensland, Australia

Cover Design – Mika Miyake

TABLE OF CONTENTS

Introduction vi	To Denise 35
Some Days vii	Kindred Feelings 36
Nature 01	Sewing 36
The Magic of the Night 01	I Care 37
The Roar of Thunder 02	New Friendship 38
Charred Blackwood 03	Lost Friend 39
The Haze of Blue 04	Wendy and Arthur 40
Joy 04	Roses from Mandy 41
The Butterfly 05	Merry's Baptism 41
Spider Web 06	My Child 42
The Wind 06	That Dress Ramblings 43
The Rainforest 07	His Life - Brevity 45
Small Grey Dove 08	Grandma and I 46
Little Things Matter 09	Powder Puff 47
Day at Rest 11	**Reflections & Musings** 48
Uluru 12	Music in My Heart 48
Oh! A Butterfly to Be 12	Who Am I 49
Sailing at Bribie 13	The Quilt 51
Nature 13	Precious Gifts 52
Cruelty 14	Guidance 52
Spring 15	Progress 53
The Lake 15	Musings 54
Tranquil Lake of Blue 15	Feelings - Touch 55
Sounds of Morning 16	Little Bird 56
Winter Ferns 16	Deep Within Me 56
Golden Girl 17	Time 57
Soul Mates 17	Smile 58
Magnolia 18	At Crossroads 59
Friends and Family 20	Balloon Rambling 60
Rag Doll 20	Mystery of Life 62
The Doll Ramble 21	Come Sail with Me 63
Angie 23	Forget about Myself? 64
Memories 24	My Cup Runneth Over 65
Teens 25	Fresh Insights 66
Share 25	Searching 67
The Tip 25	Our Feelings 67
For a Newborn 26	Enigma 68
Friendship 27	Tapestry of Life 69
For Cheryl and Greg 28	Homing Pigeons 69
Ode to Alan 29	Fresh Beginnings 70
Letter to Pam 31	Reflections on Faith 71
Relationships 32	Blessings Reflections 72
Early Reflections 33	All Alone 74
To My Son David 34	Creation 75
	Thought - Self Esteem 76

A Picture - Don't Look Back	077	Dear Jesus, Appreciate	111
On Loneliness	078	Lift Our Hearts	111
Bitter Pill, Bruised	081	Lord of Glory	112
What is Real Ramble	082	Humble	113
Prayers & Talking to God	083	Gift of Expression	113
Talking to God	083	Each Tear, Fully Alive	114
Celebrate Love	083	For Special People	115
Glimpse of Heaven	084	Hear the Music	115
Mystery	084	Jesus, Help us to Be	116
A Vision, Dark Cloud	085	Thank You - Insight	117
Grace	086	Our New Life	118
Dear Jesus	087	Reconciliation	118
Free Spirit	088	Fan the Flame - Patience	119
My Prayer for you	089	Letters to Jesus, Life	120
Found You, Lord	090	God's Promises	120
Safe Landing	090	Talk to you God	121
What If?	090	A Newborn Child	121
Turmoil, Listen	091	Bond of Love	122
A Little Prayer	091	Amazing Grace	122
Letters to God	092	Behold all Things New	123
Thank You Lord-	093	Spirit of Love,	124
Who Are We Lord?	094	I Want to be Free	125
Weary	094	Guiding Hand	125
Learning Lord - Snippet	095	A Period of Silence	126
Peace – Lord – Easter Jesus	096	Solitude is Mine	128
Our Vision Today	097	World Perspective	128
Lord, Speak to Me	097	Grief	128
Lord, Let me Listen	098	For Friends	129
Lord, Thank You	098	Love	130
Challenging Attitudes	099	Love – God in You	131
Turn It Around	099	Acceptance	131
Lord a Servant for You	099	Talking What Matters	132
A Prayer for Andrew	100	Sing	132
Chaos - Perfect	101	Compassion	133
Challenging	101	Depression	133
Perfume Sweet	102	Woman. Share	134
Help Me Lord	103	**Henrietta**	135
A Sequel	104	Tale of Henrietta	135
Thank Heavens	104	Mail Order Bride	142
Chance Meetings	105	Our Hearts Heavy	143
Be Ourselves	105	He's at it Again	145
Creativity	106	Henrietta's Head	147
My Friend	107	Facing a Foe	148
Simple Faith - My Eyes	108	Henrietta Has Surgery	149
Be Still and Know	109	She's Back	151
Love Overflow	109	George has Dilemma	154
Planned for Me	110	George is Dismayed	156
Feeling of Wonder	110	Consulted an Expert	157

George Looks Forlorn	158
False Rumour	159
Humour & Fun	161
Stiff Legs	161
Crackle	162
White Sheets	163
Oh! the Mystery	164
The Tinny Ramble	166
Ode to the Tinny	168
I Baked a Cake	170
Back to School	170
Nonsense, Little Piggy	171
A Mental Elf	172
Reflections on J.J. Poem	175
Jumping Castle	176
Oh! What Fun	177
A Group of Limericks	178
Created Not Made	179
Celebrations	181
Ode to Kay	181
My Birthday 2006	184
My Birthday 2007	184
Dance and Sing, Shame	185
Baptism	186
Pentecost Sunday	187
Joy to Your World	187
Pentecost	188
Reflections on Christmas	189
On the O Birthday	190
Christmas 2005	191
Anniversary Ramble	192
Communion	195
Christmas 1980	196
Celebrate	196
Calypso Song	197
Good Friday	198
Easter Day	198
Advent	199
Easter	199
7th Birthday	200
Christmas 2021	203

INTRODUCTION

In 2020, Kay published her book, "Ramblings and Rhyme", a collection of poetry written over the past 40 years. In addition, she had included some of the prose writings called Rambles that she sent out to friends weekly on topics dear to her heart. She donated the proceeds from that volume to Parkinson's Foundation, as she had been diagnosed many years before.

This past year, Kay's husband, Russell, came across an old folder of the handwritten poems she had penned in the early 1980s. So, it was time to create a new volume including the historical material, especially as Kay had suffered health issues and had not been able to write recently. However, here is included a poem written most recently in 2020 expressing her feelings.

SOME DAYS THERE WON'T BE A SONG IN OUR HEARTS

Some days there won't be a song in our hearts.
It is not easy to sing when the melody of life
Has been lost.
When things we have cherished
Seem gone forever…vanished in the mist of time,
leaving us lost and bereft.
Heartsick and weary, we wander in the gloom,
searching and hoping for a sign,
Something which will lead us to hope.
Now only a brick wall, silence is our companion.
As the ocean waves break upon the shore
We allow ourselves to be tossed about
In their restless dance.
How tempting it is to give in to these feelings,
To choose the easy way which leads to defeat.

However, a new day is dawning.
A glimmer of sunlight to light our way.
To rescue us from that maelstrom of water,
Which is beckoning to partner us in frantic dance.
We lift our heads in a new day.
That ray of sunshine is now a ball of fire.
It is warming our spirits.
Hearts are learning to be happy again,
Slowly we are finding the brick wall is crumbling,
The silence giving way to the sounds and rhythm of life.

Life is a forever challenge!
Happiness and contentment are sometimes there,
Sometimes not.
We should not be dismayed when perhaps, for a season,
They appear to be eluding us.
They have not gone forever ......
At times we need to recognise this.
It is the time to use our lifelines.
Our friends who are always standing there in the wings,
with listening ears and helping hands.
Do not try to do it alone; we were created for community,
To sing together the melody of life.

Kay   October 2020

Nature

THE MAGIC OF THE NIGHT

The magic of the night
The horizon is diffused with shades of colour soft.
The beauty of the sunset holds the day aloft.
A magic stillness fills the air; we dare not break the spell.
There's reverence in that feeling,
An emotion not to quell.

I feel the warmth about me as dusk begins to fade.
The evening hush unbroken,
I feel so unafraid.
The stillness blankets me in thoughts so warm and real,
Moonlight bathes my soul,
Its rays begin to heal.

The night wears on, a falling star sweeps far across the sky.
Somewhere in the distance, I hear a night bird cry.
The gentle flush of morning lights up the pale grey sky,
Until a blaze of golden light becomes the sun on high.
I rise to face the beauty and greet a brilliant ray.
Creation in all its splendour becomes another day.

THE ROAR OF THUNDER

The roar of thunder
The steady rain
Scorched brown earth,
Revives again. Grass grows green,
While cattle lean,
Can eat at will,
Content to take their fill.

Parched creek beds,
Once so dry,
Now run free,
As the wild birds fly.

The ground underfoot
Is now just mud.
The water rises, covering
Blossoms in bud.
In vain, we search
For a break in the sky.
Oh! We pray for a return
To the dry.

The creek and rivers burst,
Into flood.
Yet we in the outback,
This life's in our blood.

But when it's all o'er,
And nature has finished
Its ravage,
We stand in despair,
And question once more,
The outworking of its
Elements savage.

CHARRED BLACKWOOD

Stark against the sky it stood.
Arms reduced to charred blackwood
Night was just about to fall
On that gum so straight and tall.

In the dark, I felt its pain,
Thoughts of times gone by again.
Leaves of green with boughs that lean
Gently working tendrils seen.

Within those branches oh, so high,
One could hear the sparrow cry.
But now, no longer, could it nest,
Or bring its family there to rest.

So now all stripped to black and grey.
The tree so proud awaits the day
When then, it will no longer be,
But will live again in memories free.

THE HAZE OF BLUE

I love to see the mountains,
That haze of blue so far.
It's a feeling of awe and wonder,
That nothing will ever mar.
They speak to me of majesty,
Of strength beyond compare.
A beauty that is ageless,
Is ever-present there.
These peaks reach up –
Like arms outstretched,
To Heaven far above.
And in the foothills green, below,
Pine trees in a forest grow,
Shading them with love.

JOY

Beautiful with promise
Each day is born.
Don't turn away,
New beginnings to scorn.
For if in the morning your
Faith you employ,
Yesterday's trials
May give birth to joy.

THE BUTTERFLY   December 1982

I saw
A butterfly bright.
Colours all glowing in the morning light.

I saw...
A spider grey, fine gossamer spinning
In the cool of the day.

The butterfly fluttered, quite unaware,
The beauty afforded as it hovered there.

A sheer web hung from tree to tree.
By instinct, the spider gave beauty to me.

I saw...
You, unaware of my gaze.
As you toiled away in the noonday haze
A strand of hair, now turned grey
From a care lined brow
You pushed away.

Sometimes it seems our lives go by,
No colour abounds to please the eye.

But there is always someone there,
Who finds in us a beauty rare.

SPIDER WEB   August 1981

Spider, weave your web,
Each strand so smooth and sure.
In awe, I stand as
Silky threads,
Are woven more and more.

At last, you have perfected,
That lace of gossamer fine,
A work of art to human eye,
An offering sublime.

And so, in all its beauty,
Nature speaks to me.
The love of our Creator,
Once again, I see.

I bow before his greatness,
As in humility, I kneel.
Perhaps one day, at last, I can
Express the gratitude I feel.

THE WIND

It whispers so gently, the wind in the trees.
It plays with the flowers in the mischief of breeze,
And yet it becomes a tempest at will,
And causes havoc with all that is still.
Perhaps in its moods, it's easy to see
The action and temperament of you and me.

THE RAINFOREST   October 1983

Dappled sunlight falls
upon the path I tread.
A filigree of gold,
sheer as a silken thread.

Morning dew clings gently
to fern of forest green.
Palm fronds softly curling
As on the trees, they lean.

The murmur of the Autumn leaves,
born sweetly on the breeze.
In russet unison, they dance,
the forest glade to tease.

Water calmly sparkling
in pool of deepest blue,
Shadows and reflections
temper its brilliant hues

Lilli-Pilli bearing
the blush of early bloom
her coloured shining berries,
dispel the forest's gloom.

Fallen logs like driftwood
strewn by an unknown hand,
And mossy velvet carpet
covers rocks and shifting sand.

SMALL GREY DOVE

Small grey dove of the morning,
I hear your gentle cry.
It echoes in the morning mist,
As through the world, you fly.

Sweet slumber of the evening
Soft as a velvet gown
Stirring to your waking call
I rise from feathery down.

The fleeting hours steal away,
Inspiration you have lent.
Your presence lingers with me,
Until the day is spent.

Silent soliloquy,
The magic hours unfold.
Sunset full of beauty
Surrenders amber gold.

Across the years, you call to me
A song that will not cease,
Symbolic of the Spirit
That fills my heart with peace.

LITTLE THINGS MATTER

Little things matter.
I know that it's true.
To live in the moment,
We'll never rue!

To know the feel,
Of the breeze in our hair,
Caressing each strand
With gentle care.

To hear the rustle
Of the birds as they play,
Hearing their chatter,
What do they say?

To walk on the shore,
Collect shells borne by the tide,
To ponder what sea creature,
Has cast them aside.

Refreshed by the sea spray,
Which touches our face,
We open our spirit
And are filled with grace.

With our Universe great,
Our thoughts are as one.
As we lift our face
To be stroked by the sun.

These things oh so small,
Give pleasure, sweet.
They renew our life's walk,
Each day that we greet.

If our life is frantic
And all a mad rush,
No time for the moment
Our souls we will crush.

Rejoice in each day
Take time to just be.
The little things matter
I'm sure you'll agree.

Tiny fragments scattered
Like Autumn leaves in fall,
Across our lives, they gather.
They hold us in their thrall.

Each one is very precious.
On its own, it is unique.
Life is measured by these scraps.
Shall we take a peek?

A little scrap of this
And a little scrap of that,
A little kindness, a little love,
Shake out the welcome mat.

It is these acts of goodness,
That change our view each day.
They bring colour to our life,
In a very special way.

We need not ever worry,
That our offering is small.
Each scrap is just a little,
You don't have to give your all.

It is in this great mosaic,
Life sings beauty to our soul.
There we see each tiny piece,
Has gone to make the whole.

And so a symphony of colour,
Can be ours to greet the eye.
Just remember all the little things,
Don't dismiss them with a sigh.

Aren't you glad these acts of love,
Blessed with grace for you and me,
Are part of our Creator's plan.
Great wisdom we can see!

DAY AT REST

The day is at rest.
The time I love best.
Evening shadows fall,
Soft echoes of a night bird's call.
Then the soft mantle of night,
Holding me close until morning light.

ULURU

Clumps of spinifex are resting,
Like cushions in the dust.
Outback willows struggling
Green against the rust.

Nature's jewel set proudly,
In a crown of glistening gold
Vibrant shades caressing
Softly they enfold.

Solitary in silhouette
Shadows dare not mock
Warmly bathed in morning light
Behold the timeless Rock.

OH! A BUTTERFLY TO BE

Oh! A butterfly to be.
What joy to flit
From tree to tree.
But oh! What hazards
Can be met?
Especially – the boy,
With a butterfly net.

SAILING AT BRIBIE   April 1984

Sails in the morn,
Vibrant in hue.
Ready to challenge
The waters so blue.

Sails at noon,
Whipped by the breeze.
Foamy waves dancing
In playful seas.

Sails in the sunset
A peaceful sight
Etched on the skyline
In the fading light.

NATURE   October 1983

Nature is great
In all that she brings,
The roar of the thunder
The tinsel of wings.

The rain that falls
To drench the earth.
The butterfly emerging from
Cocoon to new birth.

So bold and so gentle,
Love sublime
Awesome creation.
Let no man malign.

CRUELTY   August 1982

Windswept coastline
Scrubby dune,
Man moving again
To an age-old tune.

One of cruelty
And one of greed,
To the cry of their victim,
They paid no heed.

The anguish and threshing
As life it defends
Mercy unheeded
For death is the end.

There was more
That happened on that day.
Butchery followed
In a terrible way.

Save the whale,
The cry of a few,
Whose love for our earth
Will ever renew.

To deplore this practice,
Is our choice.
Give us the courage
Our feelings to voice.

SPRING

Linnets singing in the park,
Help farewell the Winter stark.
Footsteps springing to the tune
As flowers dance in early bloom.
Leaves of green farewell the cold.
Spring, her beauty will now unfold.

THE LAKE   July 1982

Winter white –
Pristine pure.

Ice-blue lake –
Reflections sure.

Beauty to behold
Vivid colours, cold.

TRANQUIL LAKE OF BLUE   March 1983

Tranquil lake of blue,
Water lilies in bright hue.
Majestic swan with grace untold,
Nature before me, your beauty unfold.
Morning breeze caressing the trees.
One so caring, who all things sees,
Wonderful peace reigning within,
No other feeling to this is akin.

SOUNDS OF THE MORNING   January 1986

Sounds of the Morning
Clear and sweet,
The call of the birds
As today they greet.

I feel the new day,
Cool and still.
I let it embrace me
Til my spirit, I fill.

Enchantment I find
In the early hour
Beholding its beauty
Through each new flower.

WINTER FERNS

Skeletal ferns in shrouds of white,
Suppliantly plead in the morning light.

Stark in their pain, they cry to the dawn,
Praying for warmth as each day is born.

To no avail, their prayers suffice.
Winter's maid demands sacrifice.

GOLDEN GIRL   January 1986

I call her golden girl,
As she clambers o'er my fence.
She's strong and vibrant
And she stirs my every sense.

I can drink in of her beauty,
As I sit on my verandah.
I wish you too the pleasure,
Of a golden Allamanda.

SOUL MATES   February 1986

Soul mates,
Strong like Eagles
Soar on outstretched wings.
Through the aeons of the age,
As one, their spirit sings.

Untouched by man,
They wing their way
Across the cosmos race.
In time and space
Their souls entwined,
In heaven to find
A place.

MAGNOLIA

I will always recall
That first lovely bloom.
A gift of beauty
Shedding sweet perfume.

Her petals so perfect
Her face to the sun.
How could I let misery
Steal away my fun!

This beautiful flower,
I'd planted with hope,
A symbol, I thought,
To help me cope.

What promise it gave.
Soil and spirit gave birth.
To not rejoice,
An insult to earth.

It is a reminder to me,
Of another time,
When things were simple,
And happiness mine!

Life has many a twist,
And also, a turn.
I pray for the answer
For which I yearn.

Did I have reason
On that day?
Was there a hint
To give it away?

Did I know
That very soon,
News would be mine,
Casting a mantle of gloom?

Sometimes we wish
We didn't know.
Easier we think,
I don't think that's so!

We will face with courage,
Whatever may be.
Grace will be given
Our path to see.

Friends and Family

RAG DOLL　　February 1981

Rag doll – upon the chair.
You look so sad –
I wonder what
You're thinking there?

You used to be
So loved at home.
But now your days,
You spend alone.

No longer are you
Dressed and petted,
Nor do tears fall,
From little ones who fretted.

You were carried
Wherever we'd go.
At times we searched for you,
High and low.

To me, you hold
Stores of memories, dear.
So, my doll,
You'll ever be near.

THE DOLL RAMBLE   July 2020

Most people know about my love affair with dolls. I have many, all shapes and sizes. They sit on chairs, on beds, even hang on walls. Sadly, Russell does not share my enthusiasm, and I am sure would love to dispose of the lot. I have not bought one in some years now. However, I was flicking through the Marketplace entries on my Facebook, and I saw one that took my fancy.

It was a vintage doll and reduced to $30. I typed in a message to ask of its availability. It was still on the market, and the address was a street in Upper Caboolture. So, after our online church and virtual morning tea, we set off to collect this new find. The only problem was that I forgot to take the address. I thought I could find it on my phone. Do you think I could bring it up? No such luck!

Meanwhile, Russell's grumbles were becoming louder while I was trying to recognise the names of streets to see if they would ring a bell. I was not helped by Russell telling me that we had already wasted time driving around for an hour and a half, he had things to do at home etc. I am sure you can just imagine the comments. Finally, he says, "that is enough, we have already spent over $ 30 on petrol, and I don't really need another doll etc." However, I was determined, so I rang our daughter, Merry, who is also on Facebook and asked her could she somehow go to the site and see if she could get on to this woman. However, she needed my password. I did not have a clue as I have so many different passwords, none of which I can remember, and I have them all scribbled in my last year's diary, which of course, is most unhelpful.

Right when we had turned the car towards home, Merry rang and said she had somehow found the site, had typed in what was happening, and she gave the address again. However, she said that she had to collect her daughter from somewhere or other and would not be home for about two hours.   No way could I ask

Russell to hang around for another couple of hours - his comment was, "this is a message for you." He really thinks the universe is telling me I have more than enough dolls. Perhaps he is right.

However, I was not ready to give up. I messaged her and said I could send her a cheque or transfer the money into her bank account, so could she keep it for me, and I would collect it when I went to Noosa next. I left my phone number, however, didn't hear a word from her. Not to be deterred, I found another vintage doll, this time only $8, and it was in the same suburb where my friend Kath lives. So, the procedure began all over again. I gave her Kath's phone number so she could organise to collect it for me. When she finally phoned Kath, she said she could not find the doll and was still searching for it, all of which I thought was a bit strange. It looks as if the universe has indeed decreed that I don't need any more dolls. I'll keep you posted on this.

There is no doubt about me. It takes me a lot of words to tell a short story. I do ramble on a lot, don't I? As I've said before, being concise, sadly is not one of my gifts.

ANGIE (our visit to Nagoya castle, Japan)   April 2005

She plucked the flower,
One by one.
A posy of gold
In the morning sun.
With gentle hands
She laid them down,
On the grassy carpet.
A bright yellow crown.

Who are they for,
My darling girl?
She looked at me
And danced a twirl.

"For God, of course,"
Her answer came.
"Will He mind
they're all the same?"
She looked at me
With eyes alight.
My child, your gift
Is His delight.
He'll see the love
In every bloom
In the vases of heaven,
He'll find them room.

MEMORIES

In bed at night,
I hear the rain upon the roof of tin.
I feel now all snug and warm,
So glad I'm safe within.

I remember building cubbies,
Playing shops and all the rest.
Those carefree days of childhood.
Perhaps they were the best.

Chugging its way to the sugar mill,
The cane ferry passes by.
Sitting on the riverbank,
Loud greetings, we would cry.

Then once, to my delight,
My mother said to me,
A fancy-dress parade is "on".
A fairy you will be.

The bus ride to that old school hall,
I remember, oh! so dear.
My greatest worry was, of course,
My wings of tinsel clear.

One Easter, I remember,
The eggs my father made,
Of solid chocolate, they were shaped.
Those memories never fade!

So let us help our children,
Store up memories clear,
Of things in life so simple.
But on reflection, oh! so dear.

TEENS

These teenage years
Are quite a trial.
Have we forgotten Lord –
What it was really like?
I guess for these our children,
To do their own thing
Is the rule.
So, give us grace to love them,
And just to keep our cool.

SHARE

If on life's road
We find a friend to share the load
Then if we're both quite willing,
Our lives can be fulfilling

THE TIP

Sunday afternoons are free.
I look forward to them, you see.
Alas – alack! I have to say,
It doesn't always work my way.
For it's become for us a trip,
To take the rubbish to the tip.

FOR A NEWBORN SON   June 2008

On the day of your birth
The flags were unfurled.
Welcome small boy,
To our wonderful world.

It's a place of delight,
And there is so much to learn.
We'll all play a part,
And you'll have a turn.
The family who love you,
Your shelter will be.
Each day will bring joy,
Wonders to see.

Forever you're special,
Whatever may come.
They'll affirm you forever,
Their precious first son.

So, let's wave the flags.
We'll all celebrate
A big welcome to Jayden,
Our new little mate.

FRIENDSHIP

We sat together
Her and I.
Our thoughts were –
Just as one.

Youth and age
Together met
From nothing
Did we run.

At first, she feared
Our friendship
Honest might not be.

But our sharing
Was as natural
As any friends
Would be.

For a kindred
Answering spirit
In each other
Did we see.

I reached out
And so did she,
To touch the other's soul.
And as we did,
We helped a little
To make each other whole.

And so each of us did find,
The other true and kind.
A friendship came that day,
Which we know will surely stay.

This poem was written to farewell our good neighbours Cheryl and Greg when they moved to Maryborough.

TO CHERYL AND GREG   February 1981

Miss you – we will.
God bless you and keep you,
As each dream you fulfill.
We know he'll be faithful in all that you do.
He'll walk close beside you,
Your lives will renew.

We pray for true friendship
With folks that you meet,
In worship, in fun
And fellowship sweet.

The family of God,
Created in love,
Ever surround you.
A gift from above.

We will remember,
Happy times shared.
Sadness and laughter
As together, we cared.

So, in this new beginning,
We give our love to you.
And pray that you'll be happy
In all that you may do.

Kay was asked by the church committee to write a poem for the retirement of Rev. Alan Moore as rector at St Andrew's Anglican Church, Brisbane.

ODE TO ALAN

Dear Alan, I have been charged
With the writing of this Ode.
I have placed on my thinking cap
To help you walk this road.

Dancing in my head
Are images aplenty.
Can I use them now?
I'll try to do it gently.

You have not got a ponytail,
Nor do you sport a tat.
No piercings have been seen.
How unusual is that?

The years have passed
the time is now called gold.
Of all these things you can avail
Don't stop within the fold.

The fold to which I refer
Is the type that's really staid.
Now is the time to have some fun
Don't let the colours fade.

Don't worry what folk might say.
They're sure to tut and sigh.
It's time dear Alan for you and Jude
To kick your heels up high.

You have served us all so faithfully
Yours has been a pastor's heart.
We are thankful for your ministry
And happy to be a part.

For 28 long years, you have listened
And shared with one and all.
Stubborn at times we may have been,
But you were loyal to your call.

Little things make big things happen.
This is a fact of which we're sure.
For all the work behind the scenes
We know there is much more.

When you wake each morning,
A new challenge you will greet.
Exciting it will be.
Who knows what you will meet?

A time to spend with family
Enjoy this special gift.
Make the most of every moment
It will your spirits lift.

So, as you sail uncharted seas
We ask our God to guide,
We pray the waters will be calm
And he'll be by your side.

With gratitude we say farewell.
May love and happiness surround.
May Blessings spilling over, in your life abound.

This letter was written to Pam by Kay, trying to say the words that Emily would have said in thanks, for the kindness Pam showed to Emily while she was alive.

LETTER TO PAM

Forgive me, dear friend!
I have flown away, leaving nothing but silence.
You deserved far more than this...

Thank you for travelling with me
From the very beginning.
For walking beside me, for understanding.
And above all for showing me the
Unconditional love of our God!

I needed a shelter
Where I could feel safe as I worked
Through this transition in my life.
You helped me to find that place.

This has been a traumatic and deeply
Unsettling time for me.
My happiness in living in the gender
That I believe God has meant for me,
Has been overshadowed by negative thoughts.

Thoughts which you and many other friends
Would have read on my social media posts.
My longing for true acceptance has been deep
And troubled. Somehow it eluded me.

I have longed to be a beautiful woman.
And perhaps my desire for this has been so
Consuming that I have allowed hurtful emotions
Into my life.

Dear friend, please don't feel guilty in any way.
Sometimes when someone does what
I am about to do, friends go through
A very real time of introspection.
Many "if only" questions, like "what could I have done?"

You may think that you have failed me.
Please banish these thoughts, they are futile.
This is my decision; I cannot face the future.
You have supported me with love and compassion.
Your goodness remains in my heart.

Farewell, dear Pam, you have been a true
Friend to me,
Emily

RELATIONSHIPS   JUNE 1982

Good relationships do not just happen
Neither are they built on negatives,
i.e. refraining from doing things.
If so, they become static and do not grow.
Rather from a positive doing –
Which builds and enriches a friendship.

EARLY REFLECTIONS

I oft reflect on many things,
On love and life –
And what it brings.
Its happiness and sadness
Those times of joy and pain
I'm sure – not one thing would I change,
But live them all again.

My thoughts go winging back,
To span across the years,
When as I pass each milestone,
I shed a few more tears.

But then my mind is filled
With memories – oh so sweet.
My childhood days and feelings
I'm ready now to greet.

Feelings of running barefoot,
Along sandy ocean beach,
Foam capped waves are breaking,
Way out beyond my reach.

The rugged bush,
A lone Pandanus palm.
That old familiar feeling calls,
Of things so still and calm.

Now my senses lost in sea spray
Born gently by the breeze.
My spirit starts to dance within,
I feel so much at ease.

TO MY SON (David)   December 1980

Happiness is –
> Having a like-minded mate to play with.
> Riding a BMX Bike (mag wheels, of course)
> Spending spare 20's on pinball machines.
> Out on the waves learning the ways of a surfboard.
> Anticipating the day when he may ride a trail bike.
> Chewing bubble gum.
> Not having to have a shower and growing one's hair long.

One day the things that make a young boy happy will change. It won't be a sad goodbye – just a happy transition to another stage in his life.

Let's hope we can all remember the happiness in our childhood days – memories that even now can thrill our hearts and set our imagination on fire as we recall the fond memories of childhood days.

I wonder how our list of: "HAPPINESS IS" today would look. Would it be tangible or intangible? How much happiness do we really have today? What is contentment in our own lifestyle? Are we able to make happy transitions into the next stage of our life? Do we find new areas of happiness? Our life seems to be one of constant change – do we move with the tide or stand against it? Are we still searching for identity – or have we found it?

TO DENISE   March 1982

You make me ashamed
That I ever grumble,
Complaining of life
When you are so humble.

I know it's not easy,
That cross you bear.
How helpless I feel
I can't even share!

Pain is your partner
For most of the day.
Yet you still smile,
So little you say.

Thank you for showing me
Faith so real.
One day in His goodness
I pray God will heal.

I know close beside you,
He'll gently stay.
His love will surround you,
Each hour of the day.

KINDRED FEELING   January 1982

What is it that makes us sense
A kindred feeling in another?

It's more than instant rapport,
Rather a joyous recognition
Of mutual response.

Once our souls have met,
We've touched the stars.

SEWING

Oh! How I wish that I could sew
Great creations to bestow,
Upon my daughters young and gay
And then perhaps, in turn, they may,
From my wardrobe take their leave
My loss of clothes, I'll no more grieve.

I CARE

My friend –
Do you know I really care?
I do not understand you,
But want so much to share.

Sadness fills my heart –
As I see you sitting there –
You seem so all alone
What is the cross you bear?

Others seem to laugh,
And have a little joke
At your expense – I know.
Please forgive them –
Perhaps they've yet to grow.

Beyond the words you say
There beats a lonely heart.
I sense your cry, "accept me,"
I want to be a part.

You outwardly profess
To you, our God is dead.
My friend, your words are hollow.
I sorrow as they're said.

He has not turned away from you
He is your Father, you're his son.
His searching, caring love
Will seek you out,
Wherever you may run.

So while we pray for you
To come to Father God,
Our hands reach out in friendship,
E'en tho a different road you've trod.

NEW FRIENDSHIP   July 1982

Lord – Thank you for the privilege of meeting new people,
For bringing others into our lives,
Stimulating our thoughts
Sharing fresh experiences
Making our lives glow
In the happiness of new friendship
Thank you, Lord, for this special blessing.
Amen

LOST FRIEND   August 1982

I've lost you, dear friend.
My heart is so sad
As I think of our friendship
Good times that we've had.

I met you one day
And out of the blue
I knew we could share
That's how our love grew.

You taught me things,
That you'll never know.
I looked forward to our meetings
And enjoyed them so.

I knew you were ill
When I rang on that day,
Never dreaming
That life was slipping away.

I sorrow now
That I wasn't close by,
At least to be near you
And say goodbye.

My thoughts are with you.
I see you once more,
Not on this earth
But another shore.

You're there with the Saints,
And your friends of old
The glow on your face
A joy to behold.

I see you renewed
In every way,
And know God our Father
Is with you today.

And so our sojourn
Is fleeting on earth,
For God has promised
A gracious rebirth.

So now it's goodbye
'Til another day.
God love you and keep you
In every way.

WENDY AND ARTHUR   February 1983

Today my faith in human nature,
Surely was restored.
An act of loving-kindness
And I thank you for it, Lord.

I thank you for the person,
Who goes the "extra mile,"
Happy to share with others
And be honest without guile.

ROSES FROM MANDY

Baby's breath and rosebuds pink,
A posy sweet from Mandy.
Fragrance lingering in the evening air,
A nicer gift than candy.

MERRY'S BAPTISM   January 1985

A prayer that God
Will bless you
In a very special way,
As you share with those
who love you,
your vows afresh today.

Promises renewed and taken
As your own
We thank our Lord for
Seeds of faith
That He has carefully
sown.

So together we will celebrate
This happy day with you.
Our praise lift to Father God,
Whose love makes all
Things new.

MY CHILD   August 1982

My child – oh won't you come with me,
And walk through life in memories free.
Please take my hand as the door swings wide.
I need you now – be by my side.

Suddenly I'm young once more.
Trials of age on another shore.
I skip and dance through fields of green,
Then in delight, on an Oak tree lean.

It was here long ago
That I carved my name.
I whispered my secrets
And dreamed of fame.

Somehow the years have glided by.
No one is left to hear my cry.

The glow of youth now faded,
Those dreams yet unfulfilled.
Joy and sorrow have been mine,
And God, my fear has stilled.

My child you've helped me
More than you will know.
You've taken time to spend with me.
I hope I've helped you grow.

Through you I've walked again
The path of a faraway land.
Thank you for your patience,
And the way you understand.

THAT DRESS RAMBLINGS   November 2020

I thought I would write and tell you about a little experience that was mine a few years ago. I'm calling it "That Dress has a Story."

Many of you know that over the years, we have been lucky enough to have had many lovely river cruises in various European countries, something for which I am grateful. As our days of cruising are now over, however, we have a rich storehouse of memories to draw upon.

From that storehouse comes this memory.

We had left Marseilles and were sailing upriver on the Seine (or is it downriver) en route to Paris. It was the last day of the cruise, and when we arrived in Lyon, we disembarked and were put into buses to complete the holiday. We arrived at a lovely little walled village called La Beaume. It was almost lunchtime by the time we had enjoyed sightseeing and we were very mindful of the fact that they closed most of the shops for Siesta for a couple of hours which would mean that we would not have time to browse in the little boutiques.

Russell and I were travelling with some very nice South African friends, Lynnette and Dennis, so we hit the ground running, all going our own separate ways and organising to meet for lunch at a little coffee shop in the village. I found myself in a very nice boutique which was having a sale, and all the clothes looked very inviting. One rack had a sale sign and was marked 37 Euros, probably equivalent to about $70 I worked out (in my non-mathematical mind). I saw a little sundress - very simple, so hurriedly tried it on over what I was wearing, and it seemed to be OK, so I quickly purchased it.

Using my card and being mindful of the time, I hurried to the coffee shop where we had arranged to meet. We were all excited with our various purchases. I handed mine to Russell and said, *"here you are, take a look at what I got for half price."* He opened the parcel and, being a husband, looked at the price on my receipt first and, in a surprised tone (although it was much more than surprise), said, *"do you know how much you paid for this?"* My answer was 37 euros. *"No, you didn't,"* came the reply. *"You paid 375 euros"*. I could not believe it; however, it was true. I had paid over $500 for a dress which the original price tag would have been close to a thousand dollars, and to make matters worse, it was nothing special - just a little cotton sundress.

I grabbed the dress and made for the door, thinking I would return it. My friend Lynnette was a step behind me, she spoke fluent French and thought she could explain my error to the assistant. She tried hard, however, the shop assistant would not budge. Apparently, she said that I had bought it knowing full well what the price was, and there was no way she would allow me to return it.

It spoilt my day. I was so annoyed with myself for being so careless. Nevertheless, it was a lesson well learnt. Ever since then, I have been very careful with prices (Once bitten, twice shy). And the punch line is, it sits in my wardrobe and has been worn about three times. However, it is a reminder of my folly. It will sit there for a long time. If you know your designer labels, (which I don't), however, Mika, our lovely Japanese daughter-in-law, took one look at it and said that it is a 'Sonia Rykiel', a French designer. So, I can boast one designer dress in my collection.

So that is the end of........ "THAT DRESS HAS A STORY

HIS LIFE   June 1980

He has left home, Lord!
It was his wish
To live his life
His way.

Thank you for your word.
We know you told us the story,
Of the Prodigal son,
To illustrate more than one truth.

So, help us day by day,
To live not in bitterness and reproach,
But waiting patiently,
To joy in a family complete.

BREVITY   Christmas 1984

Reams and reams I could write.
Lovely flowery verse,
Great speeches I could plan,
And carefully rehearse.

Instead, I'll say it all
In just a word or two.
Love and peace dear Kath.
God's blessing rest on you.

GRANDMA AND I   March 1981

Small green frogs
On a May–bush white.
Newborn chicks
In the morning light.
Dark green moss
And violets of blue
Strawberries and grapes
In the garden grew.

Feeding the ducks
With milk and old crusts.
Fresh brown eggs
Collected at dusk.
Mournful sounds from
The old house cow.
Long ago thoughts
Fill me now.

Scrubbed pine table,
Laden high –
Homemade jam
And mulberry pie.

From the old table lamp,
Soft light streams.
Reflections and shadows
Add to our dreams.

Grandma and I
We sit in the glow.
Together we share
As the light burns low.

And then when drowsy
It's off to bed
In a soft down of feathers
I lay my head.

Reflections warm
Tho' nostalgic they be,
A delight to recall
I'm sure you agree.

POWDER PUFF

Powder Puff, so fluffy
Somehow seemed to be
A symbol of our mystique
Our femininity.

Reflections & Musings

MUSIC IN MY HEART

There is music in my heart.
Will you listen to my song?
Perhaps you cannot hear it,
 I've sung it for so long.

A time to give expression,
 To all that I may feel.
And yet you do not catch,
 That melody so real.

Is it that we're all so busy,
 Playing our own song,
That we fail to hear the music,
 Of the others in the throng?

WHO AM I?

Who is this person
That I call me?
I wish I really knew.
Some days I feel
That I can see
A glimpse
Of what is true.

But then there comes a cloud,
Of word and deed and thought,
All of which are contrary,
To what I have been taught.

My inner voice cries out,
This isn't really you.
But temptation is no stranger,
It's a battle ever new.

Then I really quiz myself,
As inwardly I look,
To try to understand,
The path my actions took.

And so, I struggle on,
Hoping still to find
Among the complexities of life,
A clarity of mind.

I know that there are lots of things
About me, I do not see.
Others find them easily,
Yet I don't have the key.

I know we should be able,
To face up to who we are.
But I sometimes really wonder,
If this our life can mar.

When we were created,
Each of us alone,
We developed personalities,
That we could call our own.

We often see ourselves,
Through glass of tinted hue.
Our minds show us a picture,
Which isn't always true.

But then it helps to carry us,
Through times which may be rough.
Times when we feel,
Our coping powers may
Not be just enough.

So perhaps I'm not the person
That I always think I see.
But nevertheless,
I still am glad
That I am me!

THE QUILT

She sat and stitched so lovingly,
A quilt of patches gay.
I saw her careworn face
With hair turned silver grey.
There I saw the life of yesteryear,
With through it running
Many a tear.

Her eyes were blue and gentle,
With laughter lines so plain,
Lit up with joy and gladness.
Happy times recalled again.

I saw in her a wisdom which
Is more priceless than a treasure rich.
(And so) to me, it brought reflection,
Of a life yet half gone by.
And I thought on all that still,
I fain would try.

And then I saw a picture
Of that patchwork all now complete.
Each square not overlapping,
But with the other carefully meet.
Sorrow and joy were there –
Joined oh so tenderly,
And through the framing of the years,
They brought serenity.

And so I see my life
A patchwork quilt will be.
Bright hues of golden days,
Beside the gloom of black and greys.

I will no longer ponder
On what's ahead to see,
But accept in all humility,
The plan worked out for me.

PRECIOUS GIFTS   March 1982

When the real issues of life confront us,
Strange as it may seem
The worries that once beset us,
Fade as a transient dream.

Once again, we learn to cherish
Precious gifts we share.
And be thankful for the measure
That we've been given there.

GUIDANCE

Lord, we look to you for guidance
In a world that's all perplexed.
We often lose our vision.
It's covered by a cloud.
And so we find ourselves,
Ashamed to speak for you.
Instead, become part of the crowd.

PROGRESS

They call it progress
And many folk will say,
"Of course, it cannot be,"
And look the other way.

But deep inside
A voice cries out,
Is this really what –
Life is all about?

Bulldozing our buildings,
Mellowed with age,
Taking away from history a page.
In its place, a tangle of steel,
All shining and gleaming,
With little appeal.

Oh! Where is the grace,
The romance of old?
How can we love
That edifice cold?

One day as we stand
And look for our past,
We'll realise it's gone
Buried at last.

For the powers that be,
With no thoughts have stolen,
For our heritage free
And decided that progress
Is for you and me.

MUSINGS

I have a little niggle.
It is worrying me somewhat.
A relational issue
Perhaps for you, it's not!

Are we ever guilty
Of not allowing folk - "to be"?
Is our expectation
Based on changes that we see?

The reason that I ponder
Is a friend once said to me,
Thank you for allowing
Me to be so free!

A positive affirmation
This was indeed.
Since then, I can't but wonder
How I serve my brother's need?

I asked myself
How do I interact?
Do I apply some pressure?
Could this be a fact?

Has there been temptation
To someone in my image make?
I cannot entertain it ...
It is a big mistake!

For what we guard so carefully
Perhaps not a friend would seek.
At times we want to share
Quite forgetting we're unique

The wisdom of this age
We sometimes slowly learn
To walk in another's shoes,
Helps us to discern.

So, this may be a lesson,
For us to tuck away.
Bear in mind our differences,
And respect them come what may.

TOUCH

I reach for you - a fleeting touch,
Too soon you're gone.
I need you oh so much.

FEELINGS   June 1982

Shall we go through life
Skimming the surface of our emotion?
Or shall we live our life,
In the depth of real feeling?

LITTLE BIRD   June 1982

Little bird sits in his cage.
I wonder to him if – time is an age?
He ruffles his wings, he pecks, and he eats.
To him, life's the same
Each day that he greets.

How many of us
are like that small bird?
The movements of life
Passing by unheard,
Quite content in our cage secure.
Why bother to worry
And search for more.

DEEP WITHIN ME

Deep within me
An imprisoned spirit lies.
It longs for self-expression.
How oft I hear its cries.

Sometimes so eloquent,
Whilst others with frustration bound.
Almost incoherent.
Where can the key be found?

TIME   July 1982

Time – is running out –
We often hear it said.
Today it seems to be – the pace,
By which we all are led.

Like an oxen with a ring
Around and through its nose,
We carry on – time our restraint.
Why? This question I would pose.

Like a puppet on a string,
We jiggle up and down.
Never time to smile –
More often, just to frown.

No time to hold the hand
Of that friend so all alone.
In fact, if things our steps disrupt,
We tend to really moan.

No time to sit and listen
To one whose grief would share
Instead, we make excuses to,
Why we can't be there.

No time to be alone –
To sit and just reflect
We're far too busy running
No desire to be checked.

And so then do we wonder –
When our world is full of grief
Do we question why that friend,
Let life go like a leaf?

Why families all around us –
Crumble and fall apart,
Do we ever stop to think,
Where did all this start?

Perhaps then we, the humble truth –
Might see
That little word called time,
Might well the culprit be!

SMILE

A friendly smile, a gentle touch
To the giver cost so little,
Yet to another mean so much.
Some of us are eloquent,
And although the words impress,
I somehow can't help thinking
They cost the giver less.

AT CROSSROADS

Have you ever felt
At crossroads, you are standing?
On either side, there is a tug,
Which way to go,
Is all demanding.

Our minds become confused.
There seems no clear direction.
We cannot even still ourselves,
For quiet and deep reflection.

At times there is a flash
Of insight - oh so bright.
And then a word is spoken,
And we question – is that right?

From day to day,
Our mood will change,
From soaring joy,
To deep despair,
These feelings seem to range.

People all around us,
Of this are unaware.
We hide it, Oh! so cleverly.
It's ours alone to bear.
Do we lack the courage
To make decisions clear and bold?

Others sometimes seem
To cast us in a mould.
And so their expectation is
What we focus on,
Instead of being true and turning
away from wrong.

BALLOON RAMBLINGS

Fly high, fly low?
Balloons, life, What's it all about?
Philosophical I can be
'Cause I've reached this age, you see.

I wonder, and I ponder,
As I see the future yonder.
Appealing now the past has come,
As memories flit, hours of fun.

Then we had the grace of youth.
Now a bit more long in tooth!
However, on life, we will not cheat,
Forever living to its beat.

Our bodies not as once they'd been,
Healthy, happy, somewhat lean,
Still, they serve us well.
We are still here, our tales to tell!

What about balloons, you say?
Well, perhaps that's for another day,
Maybe a symbol, an open door,
To reflect life's metaphor!

Balloons, full of air,
Buoyant flying high,
That is once my story,
I hear you sigh!
But wait! In a way,

This tale belongs to all.
We all ate at the table of youth.
We all tasted the freshness
Of that special time.

When we were full of that life-giving elixir.
Just like the balloon, how easy it is to fly high,
To feel good, to know that life is still there before you,
Even with all its ups and downs, it is there!

Now the balloon is losing its buoyancy,
The air is slowly deflating,
As the years vanish, we also diminish!
The balloon no longer is aloft but slowly
Floating to the earth.

Sometimes our descent is like this,
At others, it may be more traumatic,
It may hit with a hard bump!
However, we are not dismayed!

We have been given a great gift
The beauty of the original wrapping
May have somewhat faded,
As we peel the layers away, we may find
The colours more enduring!
We will keep unwrapping!

MYSTERY OF LIFE

A writer of old once wrote that he would rather live in a world where his life was surrounded by mystery, than live in a world so small that he could comprehend it.

Amen Amen Amen

I also choose to walk with the mystery of life! Somehow these days, I find that some of life's bigger questions are no longer as pressing as they once were. I guess I can still ask the questions; however, the answers are not as important as they once were!

Why? You may ask. I think the answer is ...Mystery!

Life is full of mystery......many questions do not really have answers, yet we keep on asking them. I find that at this age, I am content to relinquish to mystery so many things I once puzzled over.

Sometimes we can naval gaze for years when it is really not profitable. The answer is mystery. We can't solve it nor can we embrace it.

The mystery of our God

Many of us claim to have full knowledge of what is to come...I'm leaving it to mystery; after all, isn't that what faith is all about? Even though we do not see, we believe.

COME SAIL WITH ME

I'm in uncharted waters
It is a rocky ride.
I need someone to pilot me
To come aboard and guide.

I've never been this way before.
I am without a map
To chart my way when all alone.
My energy does sap.

I know that others have
Sailed these waters rough.
Each of us a different route,
Have found the going tough.

We all would love the water calm,
To navigate our sail.
It does us little good,
To against the weather rail.

We must not forget the seas
That often tranquil be
It is the time to reflect
And far horizons see.

For although diverse our ways,
We in common share
The question of our future
Together we will bear.

It is not that any would
Deny this voyage sore.
It is just the destination
Of which we are unsure.

When as a child with gusto
In Sunday school, we'd sing,
Do you want a pilot?
Our eager voices ring.

So, Lord, we invite you
To come aboard our boat.
Rescue us and guide us
That we might stay afloat.

FORGET ABOUT MYSELF January 1982

Forget about myself you say?
Impossible, I think!
Let myself go -
Drop the mask that hides each tear I blink.

To let the world out there
See who I really am
Bare my soul, expose myself,
Will they care a damn?

Perhaps if you will show me,
the love you talk about.
Forget about the words and really act it out.

Then with faltering footsteps, I'll leave myself behind
Please just keep affirming me
So my freedom I can find.

MY CUP RUNNETH OVER!

What an age it was to strive!
Would you again be 25?

Now lost in the tangle of time,
Somehow like words in a rhyme
Flitting through our mind
Verse we cannot find!

What happened in those years?
Sometimes tears.
Our life in full thrall,
We reflect and recall.

Whether happy or sad
Good or bad,
We've danced the great dance,
And sometimes by chance
We have found in another,
The love of a brother.

We've filled our days
In life's wondrous maze,
Our eyes may grow dim
Our cup full to the brim.

As we greet each hour,
May we each other shower,
With love and respect
This no one will object!

To be twenty-five once more,
Would open many doors.
However, memories are the fruit
To which we've given root!
Precious though they be
We are not bound but free!

In the years ahead
We must remember to create,
Not leave our dreams too late.
Fill our cups at the memory gate!

FRESH INSIGHT

One day it came to me
Perhaps in a moment of truth,
That somewhere along the way,
I had lost the exuberance of youth.

That precious gift, where life becomes
A challenge in all we do, had somehow vanished
And not replaced with anything new.

Instead, I was allowing life to be dull,
Quite content my feelings to lull.
Now full aware of what's happening to me,
I pray for fresh insight,
New horizons to see.

SEARCHING

I've searched and I've sought
Through years that have flown.
I've watched and I've waited
Hoping I would be shown.

But the answer to living life
As we live day by day,
Is clothed in silence.
God seems far away.

Where do I find Him?
Does he hear my cry?
Or is it just carried on the wind
With a sigh.

The mystery of life
That sweet refrain,
Will I unravel
That tangled skein?

OUR FEELINGS

Lord, help us never
To be ashamed of feelings.
That through our sharing,
We may learn
That emotion is a
Beautiful part of your creativity.
We pray that our lives
Might be open to each other,
In such a way,
That we might catch,
A precious glimpse of you.

ENIGMA

I am challenged, I am puzzled,
Perhaps you are as well.
Our eyes appear to change their lens
Wherever we do dwell.

Have you ever noticed
When travelling overseas
We ooh! And ah! At scenery,
It comes with so much ease.

We discover great new places
With excitement, we exclaim.
Distant fields seem always greener,
Home never quite the same.

I've travelled far and wide,
The wonders of our world have seen.
Yet on our doorstep find
A pearl with wondrous sheen!

Yesterday whilst walking,
A beauty worth a rhyme.
How could my eyes have missed
The splendour that was mine.

With new clarity
I saw...the river now anew.
Boats were gently bobbing.
Against the wall, the ivy grew.

The familiar so much a part
Of what we see each day,
We take it all for granted.
It need not be this way!

We need to practice open eyes
Every moment that is ours!
To live our life in wonder.
And while away the hours!

TAPESTRY OF LIFE

In the tapestry of life
Bright colours do we weave.
When gloomy times are rife
A colour comes no matter how we grieve.
A thread so fine it scarce is seen
Becomes our love, our life, our dream.

So let us strive to fill that frame
Of life that's ne'er the same
With courage and with beauty,
Although perhaps no claim to fame.

HOMING PIGEONS

Homing Pigeons
We are very much like them.
God allows us to be free to spread our wings,
But our home is always with Him.

FRESH BEGINNINGS

Sent from my iPad tomorrow when we wake, it will be the first day of our new year! Somehow, I always seem to have a sense of expectancy.... standing on the threshold of yet another beginning (even at my age.)
What about you?

Some years ago, in my diary (1991) I wrote this little reflection. It went like this...

"A new year ----a time of fresh beginnings, a time to put the things of yesterday behind and start anew.
I am reminded of our life in Christ ... A new beginning... A time to put away and forget the things that have gone before.
Isn't it a comfort to know that God not only forgives our wrongdoings, but he actually forgets them! Corrie Ten Boom says He casts them into the deepest sea and erects a sign 'No fishing.'
As a teenager in our Christian group (I.S.C.F) at school, I remember singing that old chorus."

Chapter 44: 22-23.

"God has blotted them out
I'm happy and glad and free.
God has blotted them out
I'll turn to Isaiah and see.
He's blotted them out
And now I can shout
For that means me."

REFLECTION ON FAITH BY JOYCE RUPP

I was reading a reflection by one of my favourite women, Christian writer Joyce Rupp! She had entitled it, "Trusting in God's hidden Presence" and using the verse from the Gospel of John that says, "The wind blows where it will, but you don't know where it comes from or where it goes! "

I thought that you might enjoy reading her thoughts. She says, "This reminds me of a woman who sent an old black and white photo to a photo finishing company. In the photo a man was sitting behind a cow; all that was visible of him were his feet and his legs. The accompanying note read, 'This is the only photo I have of my great grandfather. Please remove the cow so I can see what he looks like!'"

Faith is about trusting without seeing the whole picture. As much as we yearn to know and understand fully, we can only see a small part of who God is and why our life unfolds the way it does. We comprehend just a tiny portion of the meaning of events and circumstances that affect us. No matter how much we pray and study, we cannot fully explain the divine mystery that lies within and beyond us. All that is required is that we daily place our hand in the Holy One's with confidence and walk lovingly in life. We do not need all the answers, only to trust and believe that the 'Mysterious One' is as near to us as the slightest breeze or the strongest wind. Let us renew our faith in his hidden presence today!

PRAYER...Spirit of God grant that I may be at peace with that which I do not understand or comprehend. I place my trust in your constant presence!   Amen.

BLESSINGS REFLECTIONS

Blessings
Dancing, bubbling, running over
Blessings abound.
At times we do not see them,
We think they can't be found.
Even in the dark times,
They are still there.
Perhaps we cannot find them
Because our souls are bare.

Like the clouds of grey
That have a silver lining,
They are hidden for the moment,
Tucked away, still shining.
At times we fail to see them,
The culprit we may be.
We talk of blessings in disguise.
Can we make them free?

We have a blessing cup.
From time to time, we dip.
'We like to from it drink,
But merely take a sip.
We need to know,
It to the top is brimming,
Waiting there for us.
Why are we, the surface skimming?

Blessings come in many
Forms and sizes.
Sometimes we stand in awe,
And to our feet, we rise.

Some are little, some are big.
We are grateful for each one.
Don't ever take for granted,
Bless our family, bless our friends

In every way give thanks
A word in season here and there
An investment like a bank
So, count your every blessing
Name them one by one,
And we will be surprised
At what the Lord has done!
Or from them ever run!

When every day we wake
To this our wondrous world
All creation sings her song
We wave our flag unfurled
Our eyes behold her beauty
As her magic, she does weave
A miracle of God
With open hands, receive.

Every life is a blessing,
A thought to keep in mind.
We can bless each other,
And real contentment find.
Don't hold each blessing close,
In hands clasped very tight.
Open now your spirit,
It's going to feel so right.

ALL ALONE   December 1981

I gently touched his arm,
To wish him "all the best."
It was the Christmas season,
And he was all alone, I guessed.

As I gaily spoke,
I suddenly could see
The crumpled face,
The unshed tear.
In shame, he turned, from me.

He sobbed out his loneliness that day,
With cries from deep within.
His feeling was gut-level,
My heart reached out to him.

It had always been, "Hello, how are you?"
His answer had been much the same
And so I never knew the heartbreak
He'd been through.

No one had ever shown him,
Any love and care.
And so, a gentle touch,
Was more than he could bear.

For years he'd been alone,
his needs were simply met
Satisfied materially, yes!
But no affection did he get.

Grant me Lord, to see beyond
"All that meets the eye."
Man does not live "by bread alone."
So, let me hear the lonely's cry.

CREATION

A master builder,
An architect sublime?
Who planned this great wilderness
As it evolved in time.

Science gives us many answers.
It can estimate its age.
History tells the story,
Begins to set the stage.

Somewhere in the cosmos,
When worlds began to form,
When stars were flung across the sky
And night gave way to dawn.

From green of lofty forest,
To rocks on golden sand,
Our Creator blessed His world
With beauty from his hand.

He filled the mighty rivers
That flow throughout the land.
On the tiny Christmas beetle,
'He stroked a coloured band!

Each glowing shade He painted.
On a hovering butterfly,
A myriad of colour
To greet our happy eye!

With delight then He did fashion
The likes of you and me.
He looked at us with love
And then He set us free.

Father, Son and Holy Spirit,
Forever you're the same.
A litany of wonder,
All creation speaks your name!
Amen!

THOUGHT

It's the thought that counts.
What if there is naught
But thought,
No action?

SELF-ESTEEM

Self-esteem needs building.
Let's practice every day.
We need to love ourselves,
In the nicest possible way.
Friends around can help us,
By praising when its due,
And just by showing us
That they love us too.

A PICTURE   January 1986

I want to paint a picture
So lovingly for you.
Create a living memory
Of beauty through and through.

To capture on life's canvas
The things that really count,
Until at last when all complete
Then in a frame you'll mount.

This kaleidoscope of colour
That's brushed with treasures rare
The artist lays no claim to fame
It's just my life I share.

DON'T LOOK BACK

Don't look back
Across the years,
And dwell on mishaps past.
Live in the present.
Make each day
Just better than the last.
Look to the future
Full of hope,
For things to yet unfold.
And you will find contentment
And joy untold.

ON LONELINESS

Loneliness is a woman crying in an empty house! Where had she heard those words before? She remembered thinking at the time what a sad statement it was. Loneliness was a word that Barbara never thought about... An empty word, foreign to her experience!

Her outgoing nature ensured that she was usually surrounded with people, friends, acquaintances. Her life was full - full until this happened!

Where had she gone wrong? Here she was, a woman of fifty years of age, certainly not in the first flush of youth; however, looking in the mirror, she saw a trim, attractive lady, still active and anxious to enjoy life to the full. Over the years, she had had several relationships with various male friends. Never really wanting to commit to any permanence. As her thoughts flew back over that time, she couldn't help but smile...There was Felix, who panicked over the ring. He was someone she probably could have settled with if she had not made that mistake! She had found a photo in a magazine of a very beautiful engagement ring made by one of the country's finest jewellers, a 22 carat no less. Not wanting to be too direct, she had cut it out and stuck it on the fridge door, a not-so-subtle hint. Well, that was the beginning of the end. Felix did not appreciate the fact that it was not the 22 carat that she was angling for, rather the pretty design of the ring!

She was still able to smile about things that had belonged to her past, so why on earth was she aligning herself with this definition of loneliness. Perhaps she thought it was the first time that she had realised that one could be lonely even though you are surrounded by friends and even extended family.

A time for introspection - to think that she was actually that woman, alone and sitting in an empty house. Who would believe it? Self-sufficient, 'life of the party' Barbara! What would her friends think if they could see her now? The puzzling aspect was that no one thing had happened to facilitate this state of mind! It just happened! One minute she was on top of the world. The next, almost going through the dark night of the soul!

"Perhaps I'm suffering with depression", she thought, "change of life"? For once, she found herself looking into every corner of her life. "Snapshots of yesterday", she thought as her past once again came alive! Was it all about Barbara? Had she lived a selfish life? Was this some sort of lesson that life was teaching her?

It was like standing at the crossroads and working out which way to travel. She could go forward, perhaps in a new direction, or stay on that same road. The road that no longer seemed to be going anywhere. Perhaps life was challenging her to do and be someone new! She didn't have to sit and cry. It was up to her!

She was aware that these feelings had not happened overnight! It was not that she was grieving the sudden loss of a loved one, however, nevertheless, she was beginning to realise that grief presents itself in many different guises. For some time, there had been those little niggling thoughts that would come into her mind, thoughts that she would try to banish before they took hold. What did her future hold? A woman on her own. Financial security? Friends who seemed these days to be increasingly involved within their own families.

Older age was another issue that had taken root of late. Health issues could present, with no one to share, what would happen to her? Who would be there to care for her?

She thought back to the many times over the years when friends had come to her needing to talk over their thoughts and fears. Perhaps it was now her turn to seek out a listening ear for herself.

She knew that it had always been difficult for her to look to others for help. After all, wasn't she the Rock of Gibraltar to her group of friends? "Come on, Barbara, let's go for it", she said to herself, resolving that in the morning, she would make a phone call that would help her move forward.

The next morning dawned bright and sunny, she swallowed her pride, put her rock-like attitude to one side and dialled a friend. Before she had time to even think about it, she found herself sitting in a coffee shop, pouring out her feelings to a trusted friend! Why had she thought she could do this on her own. She was starting to find also the importance of getting out of the house when these feelings surfaced, to get out into the light of day. She was learning the healing power of our environment. Later that day, as she reflected on all that had happened, she thought her vulnerability had taught her a valuable lesson. No longer would she assume that happy faces translated to happy hearts. Having tasted the fruit of her misery, she would be far more aware when interacting with others.

The wonderful power of friendship for our vulnerable times, she had felt its warmth, experienced its healing power. That day she felt that life had taught her a valuable lesson!

THOUGHTS

Contentment we seek,
But if we're not wise,
Avarice comes,
In careful disguise

I sometimes feel,
Life is like a jigsaw puzzle.
We have to find that missing piece,
Acceptance and then trust.

BITTER PILL

It's a bitter pill to swallow,
When life becomes unfair.
But if in pity you would wallow,
No joy will you find there.

BRUISED

You bruised my spirit,
With your words
That were so cruelly spoken.
Perhaps you now will realise,
Why my love is token.

.

WHAT IS REAL RAMBLE   APRIL 2015

On Sunday we have our first pastoral care meeting for the year. How important it is that we show our love and care for each other, especially in our church family.

One of my favourite coffee mugs shows an illustration of a rather shabby little donkey with the caption:

" That which is loved is always beautiful!"

This little saying is an old Norwegian proverb. It reminds me of "The Velveteen Rabbit" in which the rabbit and the skin horse have a conversation about what is real.

"What is real?" asked the rabbit.
The skin horse answers:
"Real isn't how you are made, it is something that happens to you, when a child loves you for a long time, not just to play with you, but really loves you, then you become real."

Rabbit: "Does it hurt?"

Skin Horse: "Sometimes when you are real, you don't mind being hurt! It doesn't happen all at once…you become. It takes a long time, that's why it doesn't happen to people who break easily, have sharp edges, or have to be carefully kept. Generally, by the time you are real, most of you has been loved off, your eyes drop out, you get loose in the joints, and very shabby. Those things don't matter because once you are REAL, you can't be ugly except to people who don't understand!"

So often children's stories speak to us about the really profound things of life. Loving one another as Jesus has asked us to do, can help each other to be beautiful, become real.

PRAYERS and TALKING to GOD

TALKING TO GOD - REFLECTION

Lord, I am glad it is you who is judge of all the earth.
If left to us, there'd be a lack of Heavenly Saints,
To love and praise your name,
For we who are so human, just love to mete out blame.

But you, Oh! Lord are truly great
And know our feeble hearts.
You look beyond our actions
As new life your grace imparts.
Amen.

CELEBRATE YOUR LOVE TODAY   January 1986

Lord, I want to celebrate your love today,
not in partying,
not in singing or in dancing,
But just in the quietness of this hour.

I lift my hands to you and meet you in
The fellowship of The Holy Spirit.
Amen.

GLIMPSE OF HEAVEN   January 1981

I felt very close to you, this morning Lord –
I guess you knew it too.
It was almost as if – for a brief second,
I caught a glimpse of heaven.

I can't describe the feeling that came to me.
Perhaps one way to try and express it,
Is - sheer happiness,
Rather like the feeling one has on -
a warm spring day,
When everything is peaceful,
Skies are blue – that cloying honey sweetness fills the air,
That intangible emotion of utter contentment.
To me, this morning, that was heaven.
Thank you for moments like this.

MYSTERY   October 1981

This world is full of mystery –
My quest will never end –
Until that day – Oh God –
Your final blessing send.

A VISION   October 1981

Take the blinkers from my eyes,
That I may truly see,
A vision so unlimited,
A mind that's truly free.

Lip service shall not be given,
To that, I've not thought through.
A daily challenge prayed for,
Dimensions ever new.

DARK CLOUDS   January 1982

Yesterday life was a celebration .... happiness was mine.
Today, the joy has gone, and sorrow fills my soul.

Dark clouds of gloom
have banished my bright and shining sun.

I no longer live, rather endure.
The challenge of each day is lost.
Magic moments have gone forever.

Across the dark abyss of time,
My weary footsteps seem to drag.
I'm even denied the sweet solace of sleep.

In the wilderness of my pain, I cry out to you, Oh God.
Hear my prayer, quieten my soul.
Out of the brokenness, restore in me your perfect wholeness.
Take me by the hand and lead me back to life.

GRACE   January 1982

Lord, you are so good to me –
I wonder why?
You suffered and hung on Calvary's tree.
You knew for sin you'd die.

I know I'm not deserving,
Of the love you gave that day,
And yet unworthy as I am
It was the only way.

And so my dearest Saviour,
Although I ponder still,
I accept in thanks your wondrous grace.
My life is yours to fill.

You took time to be alone –
And from the crowd withdraw.
It was there in solitude you prayed,
And God, your Father saw.

He saw the longing and the need,
To commune with Him apart,
Sharing together the burden,
Of a heavy-laden heart.

And so, Oh Lord –
Amidst the clamour
Of life from day to day,
We long to find our Father,
In just the same quiet way.

To bring to Him our doubts and cares
And talk with Him alone,
To sense His gentle presence
In the way that you have shown.

DEAR JESUS

There is so much I want to talk to you about! At times I just need to pour out the needs of my heart. Thank you for listening.

As I was working this morning, I was thinking about our individual weaknesses and how reluctant we are to allow others to see our shortcomings in certain areas.

It occurred to me that, in fact, it would probably be helpful if we were comfortable enough to share these things. What a relief not to have to be the "super strong Sally" at all times .... ..how much more effectively we might relate to each other. More importantly still, how much closer we may become to you. After all, wasn't it the Apostle Paul who wrote that in his time of weakness, your answer to him was,

"My grace is all you need, for my power is strongest when you are weak."

Yours in weakness
Kay

FREE SPIRITS January 1983

Today I walked in another world
Flying aloft freedom's flag unfurled.

The streets, to me, were
Paved with gold.
To think these eyes could
Such wonders behold.

The church I passed, bells
Tolled in praise.
People were talking,
Unaware of my gaze.

Once again, I knew it was spring.
Oh, just to hear the small birds sing.
Ears that once were dulled with pain,
Now anew heard their sweet refrain.

No more did I whisper
Afraid to express
Anger within and
Deep distress.

To write without censor –
My words to erase
These wonders so new
Never ceased to amaze.

Do you who are there
these wonders to see,
Know what we would give
Free spirits to be.

MY PRAYER FOR YOU   January 1982

I cannot be there with you,
To comfort and to share
To put my arms around you
To show how much I care.

And so each day I bring you,
Before our Father God –
He sees and understands your grief
That path He's also trod.

I thank Him that you are his child
And for His love to you.
I pray that you will feel His presence
In all that you may do.

I know He'll gently lead you,
Back through that valley low.
He only asks we trust Him,
Because He loves us so.

I ask Him to walk beside you,
Each moment of the day
Until the greyness of each hour
Becomes a shining ray.

I pray that blessings from above
Will fall like gentle rain,
Until that day when memories dear
Will hold no grief or pain.

FOUND YOU LORD

So, I found you, Lord.
You spoke across the years.
I met you as the Saviour,
Who takes away all fears.

We do not have to search
In places far away.
Instead-
You come to meet us
Just where we are today.

SAFE LANDING

When I'm flying high
Lord,
Help me to land safely.

WHAT IF   June 1982

What if my life is o'er,
And I still haven't found who you are?
Or – sadder still who I am?

TURMOIL (Decision Making)   June 1982

Lord –
My mind's in a turmoil –
Please stem the flow,
Of thoughts that are
Rushing to and fro.

I feel in a panic
I want to be still.
Just calm me and
Help me to find your will.

LISTEN   June 1982

Lord,

You've shown me just how important it is that I take time to listen to others, to hear what they're really saying. Please help me to remember then how important it is that I take time to be still and really listen to you.

A LITTLE PRAYER

Forgive us, Oh! Lord
If we lift your name high,
But fail to be moved
By our brother's cry.

LETTERS TO GOD   January 1982

Dear Jesus,

Running away never did solve anything, did it? And yet I seem to remember many of our great heroes in the bible trying it!

But if I'm right, it didn't help their problems either!

l especially think of Elijah! Elijah that great man of God. You had given him such victories...even now I can picture him...up on that mountain with the prophets of Baal, so full of courage and confidence in you.

And then so soon after to see him fleeing from Jezebel. He was actually running away. He was afraid!

You know Jesus that really encourages me; if that great Prophet of God could get cold feet and run and hide when the going was tough, and still you were with him, then I am comforted by the knowledge that no matter what I do or where I go, you are there.

Through all my doubts and fears, my times of running and turning away, You will not desert me.

And so dear Jesus, whether you speak to me in the roar of the thunder or like Elijah in the gentle whisper of the breeze, I will wait and listen,

Amen.

THANK YOU, LORD   January 1983

Lord,
I want to say, "thank you"
This morning for this friend,
I've just received a letter from.

Sometimes it's just that friendly
Message from another that
Can lift our troubled hearts.

To know that someone,
Even though she be many miles
Removed, cares about us.

What comfort dear Jesus that can be.
I sit down and as I read,
I can almost see her smiling face.

Thank you for her wonderful gift of writing,
That stirs my imagination and,
Takes me into her life.

For a time, I'm able to
Forget my worries –
Somehow, she has sensed my need.

Thank you again, Lord
And please bless my dear friend.

WHO ARE WE, LORD? February 1983

Who are we, Lord?
If not a product of all
We see, hear, and do?

Surely to enable us to give out
We must first of all,
Take in of that which
Is all about us.

How influenced we are by
The opinions of others
The written word,
the experience of life itself.

Help us to sift and resift
This precious material
Which shapes our lives –
So that we may discard
All that is irrelevant
Keeping that which is truth and beauty
and express it accordingly.

WEARY

Weary I am
In body and soul.
Renewal I seek
To make me whole.

LEARNING, LORD   February 1983

Lord – I'm still trying to learn
Just how to accept compliments graciously.

Is it part of really learning,
To love myself – accepting
Me as I am?

How easy it is to brush
People off with the usual
"cliches".

(A very unloving action
On my part)

So please, by your Spirit,
Grant me the extra grace
I need to just say
"Thank you".

SNIPPET

Evening's light
Morning's glow.
Thank you, Lord
For making it so!

PEACE   March 1983

You gave me
Peace in the evening
When my heart was
Heavy and sad,
From the cares of this world.
You lifted me
And again I was happy and glad.

LORD   1983

Lord –
Please forgive me for these feelings of frustration – of anger. Help me to see the underlying cause, so that I may come to terms with the real problem.

DEAR JESUS - Easter 1983

All at once, I know how the Hymn writers of old felt when they wrote of the "inexpressible joy".

Today is Easter morning, and You are present in your resurrection power. Of course, Lord, You are always with us, but somehow this morning, the reality of it is just so great.

The stone has rolled away, the women no longer mourn.
You have risen.
Hence Angels sing – Alleluiah, Alleluiah.
    Amen.

OUR VISION TODAY   October 1983

Our vision today
May limited be.
Let's pray tomorrow,
New insights we'll see.

LORD - SPEAK TO ME   January 1985

Lord,
Speak to me in the breath
of the breeze,
As it skims the waves
In restless seas.

Speak to me in the gentle shower,
Raining new life on
Each weary flower.

Speak to me in the heat
Of the sun,
Warming my spirit so we
Become one.

Speak to me as I ponder
Anew,
Your plan for my life.
How best to serve you.

Speak to me so that
I may hear
Your voice o'er the tumult,
Loving and clear.

LORD LET ME LISTEN January 1985

Lord, let me listen
Not go my own way.
I'm tempted to wander.
Please help me not stray.

I've yet to unravel,
The skein that is spun.
There are moments when
I want to turn and just run.

Times when I feel
We're playing a game,
As we sit in our churches,
Praising your name.

Forgive us, Oh Lord
If your name, we lift high
Yet fail to be moved
By our brother's cry.

LORD, THANK YOU January 1985

Lord, thank you for those marvellous people that we can feel really comfortable with. That happy relationship where we can be ourselves – forget pretence, let our masks drop and just relax.

Thank you for their wonderful ability to put us at ease – for their love and acceptance. Bless these dear friends.

Amen.

GOD CHALLENGING MY TRUE ATTITUDES
                              January 1985

Do I really act out what I speak?

Can, and do I really love the unlovely?

Can I offer them my hospitality in the same way that I can share with someone who is pleasant and easy to be with?

Do I give of myself in this way, having the same love Christ had (He was never ashamed of anyone)?

That old Hymn comes to my mind "Am I ashamed to own my Lord – or to defend His cause?" Remembering that Jesus said,

"If you give a cup of cold water in my name, you give it unto me". Can I treat everyone as I would Jesus? No excuses – no justifying.

TURN IT AROUND   February 1985

Turn it all around.
Sift it carefully through.
And then perhaps you'll find,
The Lord will challenge you.

LORD

Keep me from feeling "I know it all."
Help me to be humble so
That I may be an effective
Servant for you.
"Amen"

A PRAYER FOR ANDREW   May 1985

He is my first child, Father God,
Born all those years ago.
A downy, curly head who
Came in Winter snow.

Often mischievous and naughty,
Through the passing of the years.
My memory's not so dim,
That I've forgotten all the tears.

In teenage years the quiet despair
When life's choice seemed all awry.
But now on looking back,
We're glad we let him try.

And now today, another fork
Upon the road of life.
I pray that he will walk the way
That leads away from strife.

So bless him now, Dear Lord,
As he travels far from home.
Please walk close beside him,
Wherever he may roam.

OUT OF CHAOS

Out of chaos came order.
From darkness came light
Yesterday's blindness, now blazing sight.
The word of creation spoken aeons in time,
Forever ongoing, in your life and mine.

LORD, YOU'RE CHALLENGING ME   January 1986

Lord, you're challenging me again!

Right when I was feeling pretty comfortable, the road stretching ahead smooth and straight. Suddenly the stones have appeared, and the going is rough. I'm tempted to ask why? But I guess I know the answer. For now, there's a bend in the road, a change of direction - a new path to be travelled.

But thank you, Lord, the destination has not altered.

PERFECT

Lord – none of us are perfect,
Though sometimes we appear,
To think that way.
Grant us humility,
And a great sense of humour,
To see ourselves as we really are.

PERFUME SWEET

Perfume sweet of blossom bright,
Winter repents in spring's new life.
Skies that once were black and grey,
Cloudless now in a bright new day
Seeds buried deep in the earth so bare,
Greet new life – nature's gift so rare.

Thank you, Lord, in our life so short
In the cycle of seasons, a great truth you've taught.
For when we've lived this winter through,
We know you've promised our lives to renew.

Springtime will come as never before.
It's presence and beauty in love you'll restore.
For just as each plant dies to give birth.
So, Lord, our bodies return to the earth.

JUMBLED THOUGHTS

Inside of me I feel
Many a jumbled thought.
Just help me sort them out
That I may express them as I ought.

PEACE

If peace eludes us –
Perhaps we're looking in the wrong places?

HELP ME, LORD!   January 1986

I need to share your love
Today with a friend
And it's not easy.

It's not that I don't want to,
But forgive me, Lord,
Where do I start?

I've got to be honest –
I've read all the books
Listened to all the preaching
And still, I'm uncomfortable.

Oh, Lord! I cry out
To your Holy Spirit
To flow through me now,
Filling me with your
Love and power.

So that I may generously
Give of myself
And share you with
This dear friend.

Amen.

A SEQUEL TO MY LAST PRAYER   February 1986

Lord

I have worked out that this troublesome pride of mine, obviously has something to do with my inability to share.

You see, I don't want people, especially certain people, to think I'm a fanatic — a crackpot.

After all, I do have an image to preserve.

See what I mean, Lord! So please start with me first—minister to my hang-ups. Help me to sort out my mixed-up thoughts, so that I can be an effective witness for You.
Amen.

THANK HEAVENS LORD   January 1986

Thank Heavens, Lord,
That at long last
I'm learning to be
Comfortable with me.

Isn't it great when suddenly,
All the doubts and
Uncertainties fade away,
And that glimmer of light
Bursts forth into sunshine.

Right now, I feel
I know who I am
And where I'm going
And it's just so good
To be me.

CHANCE MEETING   February 1986

Lord, thank you for chance meetings!
The opportunities you give
Us to minister to someone who
Has a need.
Perhaps just a kind word,
Or shoulder to cry on, or just
A listening ear.
Help us to have your
Wisdom, your empathy, remembering
That you were the great counsellor.
Amen.

BE OURSELVES

Lord, I want to talk to you.
How far can we really go,
In "doing our own thing?"
When does this action,
Turn from independence
Into selfishness.
We know that in
All that we do,
Some influence –
Whether good or bad,
Reaches out to touch others
Close to us.
I just pray – that
In the midst of
Wanting to be ourselves,
We don't lose sight,
Of who we really are.

CREATIVITY

Lord -
Thank you for wonderful creative
People down through the ages,
Who have stirred our
Hearts and thoughts
Through the written word.

For imagination which has
Lifted us from the hum-drum of our
Everyday existence into the
Fascinating world of make-believe.

Kaleidoscopes of colour
Vividly imprinted on our minds
Words that make our
Hearts sing.

We thank you for
The beauty and majesty of poetry,
High adventure in narrative,
Poignancy, laughter and joy,
Exciting biographies where,
We've found inspiration through
The lives of others.

Thank you for these people
Who share themselves with us.

We pray that as we read, we
May absorb a little of that same
Imagination and beauty that our
Lives may be enriched. Amen.

MY FRIEND

Lord –
I just bring my friend before you this morning. Thank you for your love for her and the comfort that she draws from it. But dear Jesus, how sad her heart is.

She is a very new grandmother and just aching to hold this little new life in her arms. Her son and daughter-in-law are afraid the babe will be spoilt and won't allow her this joy.

Father, the young are so idealistic, trying hard to do the right thing.
But how we would pray for a softening of their heart?
Just bless this little family, Lord.
Help them to see this hurt and open their eyes
to the love that is there.
Amen.

SNIPPETS

Acceptance and then trust.
Help us, Lord
To find in mutual friendship,
These basic ingredients.

When we feel a "blob" Lord, help us to get ourselves together.

SIMPLE FAITH

Lord, I yearn for a simple faith,
Uncluttered by the rules of man.
For then, I know your Spirit
That fire of love will fan.

For whilst I buffet to and fro in the tangled skein of life,
It's hard to hear your voice,
Above the clamour
And the strife.

Just as a little child
Grant me a simple trust.
For it will last forever,
While man's words will turn to dust.

MY EYES

You opened my eyes
My soul danced.
Thank you, Lord
For new dimensions in faith.

BE STILL AND KNOW THAT I AM GOD

Lord forgive me.
I must confess,
I have forgotten what it's like
To just be still.

To sit quietly and to feel your presence.
Forgotten how to listen for the still small voice.
Forgotten Lord that we were made for fellowship with you.
That you delight in me as I in you.

Forgotten what it's like
To feel that tender love.
That understands
when others can't.

So, dear Lord, restore in me,
The need for sweet communion,
So that once again I meet with you
And know that you are God.

PRAYER

You filled my heart with love overflowing.
How long I'd searched Oh! Lord for this.
I knew as never before the true meaning,
Of grace undeserving.
You set my spirit free to worship you.

PLANNED FOR ME

Sometimes I want to know,
Just what's in store for me.
I'm glad – so glad – Oh Father,
You've planned that's not to be.
So, when in this mood you find me,
Just gently take my hand,
And lead me through that day
And help me understand.

FEELING OF WONDER

Oh Lord, give me words to express,
This new feeling of wonder that comes from above.
You helped me to see that faith, all-embracing,
Is the need for our world in the times so frustrating.
But Father, you showed me as well,
That each of us carries your spirit within.
So let us each one be willing to see
Yourself in the other – till Eternity.

MY ANGRY SON
Hold him close, Lord
He is yours.

DEAR JESUS, APPRECIATION

Isn't it important to appreciate each other? Of course, the whole problem is that we often do, except that we never begin to open our mouth to tell each other so.

I guess this train of thought really started, after sharing with good friends, the very happy wedding of their son. It was one of those lovely old-fashioned weddings, of speeches etc., and everyone obviously having a great time.

It was Russell's privilege to propose the toast to the groom's parents, and then, of course, they responded. Perhaps for the first time in many years, we had a wonderful opportunity to verbalise our appreciation of each other. Certainly, during that time, I'm sure we had expressed those feelings in many different ways, but how much nicer to tell each other.

So dear Jesus, help us to affirm each other by learning to just tell our friends how much we really value them as people, and what it has meant to us to have them contribute to our lives.

In appreciation,
Kay

LORD, LIFT OUR HEARTS

Help us to remember that there is no dividing line between the spiritual and the secular. That all we do should be an expression of your life and love.
Lift our hearts, that all may be to your glory.
Amen

LORD OF GLORY

You are the Lord of Glory,
Yet Shepherd of the fold
Gentle, caring Father mine,
Whose love is still untold.

I cannot fully comprehend
How great you really are,
At times I feel so close to you
At others, I'm so far.

I know that when we walk with you,
Your Spirit comes in power.
Thank you for this blessing
That you so freely shower.

In confidence, I come to you,
Knowing You will hear my prayer.
Your will be done, my heart cries out,
As joyously we share.

Infinitesimal as I am,
you've made no other the same.
You - My Father - Lord of Glory,
Have called me by my name.

HUMBLE

I talked about sin,
How condemning I must have been.
Until, Oh Lord! You showed me a truth,
I had not seen.
So please forgive me
those words harshly spoken.
Make me humble,
That I may be
Willing to be broken.
Hold my tongue,
From making judgements which,
Should not be mine.
For Lord my God,
Judgement alone is thine.

GIFTS OF EXPRESSION

Dear Jesus,
Thank you for the gift of expression!
Over the last weeks and months, I've come to realise that many of the issues that I have verbalised with you have actually become realities in my own life!

How much strength I have gained from the experience of talking them over with you.

In some way, it seems I have already started to come to terms with some of the problems and, with the help of your Spirit, have the confidence to begin to deal with them.
Thank you, Jesus

EACH TEAR

Father God, you number the hairs upon my head.
You even see each tear which in solitude, I've shed.
You hang the stars that sparkle across the evening sky
And a golden ball of fire to be my sun on high
Nature all around me sings your eternal love.
From the mountains in the distance,
To the floating clouds above,
You fill my life with beauty.
It will never be the same.
Do you wonder that I marvel,
And praise your Holy Name?

FULLY ALIVE

Thank you, Lord, that we can be "Fully Alive,"
Aware of self, of others,
Life, the world around us,
And above all else,
Aware of you.

Thank you that wrong vision,
Mistaken attitudes,
Can be recognised and –
With your help, overcome.

Thank you that we can come to terms with
Our own selves as
Your very human people.
Recognising our inadequacies but also
The great potential you see in us.

PRAYER OF THANKSGIVING FOR SPECIAL PEOPLE

Lord...
Thank you for those who are warm,
And generous of heart,
Who teach us lessons that,
We could never learn on our own.
Those who have so little to give,
And yet give so much.
In fact, in many ways, their lives,
Are wrapped in love,
Treasures that are intangible,
Life has blessed them in full measure.
Grant us the humility to meet you afresh,
In the lives of these special people.

PRAYER

If you hear the music, join the singing.

Lord, help me to always hear the music
— the symphony of your love.

Grant that on hearing, I will joyously,
Join in the great song.

What a tragedy to turn our backs,
On the music of life

LETTERS TO JESUS

Dear Jesus,

I want to live for you,
Be your friend.
Honesty will be important,
I'll not pretend.

I guess there are always times, even in our spiritual lives, when we are tempted to pretend that we are somebody we're not. Perhaps pride has something to do with this. We are afraid that people might see that we don't quite measure up to their expectations. Please note, Dear Jesus, that I did say "their expectations". Not yours.

One positive thing I have found as I grow older is a sense of becoming more comfortable with myself. I have been learning who I am, where I am going, accepting my faults, unreached goals, and somehow still feeling, "It is good to be me".

Sometimes I have a sneaking suspicion that even though, as Christians, we talk a lot about acceptance, we often fall by the wayside when it comes to putting it into practice. It is not always easy when we start to communicate honestly in our relationships, as not everyone will be able to cope with us being ourselves.

Help us to be people who dare to be what we are, who do not want to be liked at all costs, and one day can stand alone before You with head held high.
Amen.

LETTERS TO JESUS

Dear Jesus,

I've just had a very humbling experience!

Today I have visited some very elderly folk who are virtually "shut-ins." As I spoke to them, I suddenly began to realise that I've been guilty of becoming self-righteous, almost patting myself on the back for my "good works."

But Jesus, you do have a habit of "bursting the bubble," when we start to get a little too full of self.

Driving home, I suddenly saw in my mind the most marvellous basket of bread, loaves of all shapes and sizes, iced buns, cakes, all the most mouth-watering goodies one could imagine.

From that exciting assortment, these elderly friends had been given nothing but the crumbs. Could you believe it, Jesus?

I had given them the crumbs from my overflowing basket, and I even had the effrontery to feel good about it.

Thank you for this very valuable insight. You gave your all, and yet how often we are content to give so little of ourselves.

Yours in humility,
Kay

LETTERS TO JESUS   December 1984

Dear Jesus,
This morning I was thinking about the new life we have in you.
We never seem to talk about it much, and yet it is the most
Precious gift that we will ever have.

Thank you for your great love, which made it all possible,
Forgiveness and the wonderful promise of eternity with you,
The beautiful assurance that we have within.

And yet it is even more than that; a day to day walk with you,
A deepening friendship, a sharing together. You, always aware
Of our needs, our doubts and fears.

Thank you for a heightened sensitivity to all around us:
the beauty of a sun-filled day,
the fragrance of flowers in bloom.
A lone petal floating on the water,
and the gentle breeze in the trees.
A feeling of oneness with each other,
with your love and peace flowing between.
Amen.

LORD

Help us to have,
A ministry of reconciliation.
Just as you became a bridge,
Between God's holiness
And man's sinfulness,
Help us to span the distance,
Between us and our fellow man.

LETTERS TO JESUS – FAN THE FLAME

Dear Jesus,
They're hungry,
and I am satisfied.
The pangs I feel -
do not hurt.
I'm complacent
yet don't want to be.
I cry out for justice.
I want my involvement to be real,
But somewhere along the way
the enthusiasm wanes.
Oh! yes! ... I still feel compassion,
deep sorrow
But where is the spirit of yesterday,
That burning zeal, I want to help Jesus?
Please fan the flame,
don't let the fire go out.

PATIENCE AND LOVE

Lord, we can't all
Walk at the same pace.
You never expected us to.
So help us not to put
distance between each other,
But to live together
In patience and love.

LETTERS TO JESUS

Dear Jesus

Adorning my refrigerator is a small "scroll" magnet given to me by a friend... it bears these words...

> "I can complain because rose bushes
> have thorns
> or rejoice because the bushes bear roses."

What an encouragement! How often we can apply this to our own experience. Times when the thorns of life leave us hurting as they prick again and again, with the sharp point of disappointment and rejection.

Sometimes we feel as if our lifeblood is being drawn from us, as they draw our tears and scar our yesterdays.

However, tomorrow is always dawning; we celebrate a new day and the fragrance of its bloom. We know that God's promises are new every morning so that we can say yes to life and rejoice in the roses.

LIFE

Life is a learning process.
Oh, God, Help me
Never to forget.

TALK TO YOU GOD

I want to talk to you, God
not in great long prayers,
Just you and me,
I want to tell you how I feel,
how I really feel,
Just a good old down to earth talk,
Let me share my happiness,
my sadness,
my fears, my troubles.
I want to be myself.

A NEWBORN CHILD

A newborn child
What joy! Real joy!
A prayer of thanks
For this little boy.

How we marvel
At our Creator's hand.
A miracle on earth,
This wonderful birth.

And Lord, it takes us back
In time and space,
To that happening,
In a very humble place,
Where you the Lord of all
Became to us,
A reality,
Of our Father's love and grace.

BOND OF LOVE

You are my friend.
You're always there,
Especially when
My soul I bare.
Yet I have never told you
In words so real and true,
How precious is the bond of love
That I can share with you.

DEAR JESUS

There are times when, after having done something for one of my children, I hear myself saying, "You really don't deserve it."

Today the words had hardly passed my lips when You gently spoke to me.

"That's what I did for you, my child; you did nothing to deserve it."

I breathed a prayer of thanks for this gentle reminder.

Our new life in Christ is surely Amazing Grace, and yet difficult sometimes for us just to reach out and claim this precious gift.

A gift born out of love that we can't even begin to comprehend …the unconditional, unfailing love of the Father. A love that he accepts us just as we are …A love in which we lose our life, to live gloriously in the life of Your Spirit.

Yours thankfully,
    Kay

BEHOLD I MAKE ALL THINGS NEW   January 1985

Praise the Lord for our new life in Jesus.

Suddenly this morning, the words of that old, old revival hymn came into mind.

"Are your garments spotless, are they white as snow, are they washed in the blood of the lamb?"

Perhaps the reason for this is that since Sunday, I've been thinking of that lovely illustration of Jesus being our righteousness, clothing us in His wonderful garment or robe of goodness.

I was reminded of the day when I tried so hard to remove a stain from my daughter's dress. I really rubbed and scrubbed at that spot, hoping not to have to wash the whole garment. All I succeeded in doing was to make it far worse, finally having to launder it completely. How much precious time would have been saved if I had done that in the beginning. How easy to be wise after the event!

Perhaps that's how many of us are in our Christian lives. We try so hard to just remove the spots from our garment "figuratively speaking," instead of realising it just won't work. Our garments or lives have to be made new, not through any self-effort, and the only way that this is possible is by allowing Jesus, to create in us a new heart.

As the psalmist said, "Create a pure heart in me, Oh God, and put a new and loyal Spirit in me."

Kay

THE SPIRIT OF LOVE

Thank you, Lord,
That we can express
Our worship in so many ways.

You have given us so many forms,
In which we can show -
Our love to you.
We can laugh, dance and sing
Offer our all to you.
And you accept it!

Accept it – because you see,
The Spirit of love,
Which prompted it.

So let us not be afraid,
To offer you our senses
In sheer spontaneity.
Then we are really ourselves.

THE LAMB

I love the story, Lord,
Of the lamb that went astray,
Because I know there comes a time
We all will wander – come what may.
So, thank you for your promise,
Of love and faithfulness,
That brings us back within the fold
And rejoices in happiness.

LORD - I WANT TO BE FREE

Lord, don't let me be pushed into a mould. Do you know what I mean? The feeling of conforming to someone else's set idea of creed and belief.

Lord, I want freedom to move. To be myself with you, not to have the thought patterns of others, superimposed on me...I want to find you on my own level, in the way that you have planned for me. Responding to you in the way in which I feel comfortable and free. At times, each of us find new dimensions of faith, experiences where together with you, we can explore and share new insights.

And so, Lord, I pray that I may be always open to the fresh wind of your Spirit, in whichever way it may blow, is that of yours alone.

GUIDING HAND

Lord, help me to get myself together
In the business of life
Let me make decisions
Which lead away from strife,
So that in the days to come
I might look back and see
How loving was your guiding hand,
Ever reaching out to me.

A LETTER TO JESUS - AFTER A PERIOD OF SILENCE

Dear Jesus,

It is a long time since I last wrote a letter like this to you. Some years ago, I would very readily put pen to paper expressing a whole gamut of emotions, anger, joy, petty annoyances etc. You were the one person who understood. I would pour out my feelings and leave them safely in your keeping.

Forgive me for my silence…thank you that you never give up on us even when sometimes we seem to give up on you—times when life seems to take over with all its busyness and complexities. Even David in the Psalms speaks of being conscious of faults that defeated him. He knew Your forgiveness which leads to victory.

There is so much that I am grateful for…this letter could have no end. (One consolation is that you don't have any problem deciphering my scrawl). This morning I just want to focus on my wonderful friends, both old and new… people whom you have graciously brought into my life. What a great gift you have given me. Through them, you have showered your love and blessings on me in a special way. How these friendships over the years have enriched my life, helping me in so many ways to be the person I am today.

I can even say "thank you" for the negatives. We do feel that some people are a bit scratchy at times (myself included). Nevertheless, this has also been a time of learning and growing. In the process of 'becoming'…becoming what, you might ask? I'm still grappling with that as well. I want to become more and more the person you would like me to be. Many times, we read that we need to conform to your image...I figure that means being spiritually mature, a well-rounded person (now, don't laugh - "well-rounded" in my case would be an apt choice of words). A whole person may better express it.

I praise you for our little group of women who have met together over the years...for our shared love of you and each other, binding us together and providing support and friendship. I am thankful for the readiness of friends who listen (to the grumbles as well as the joys) for their wise counsel and, above all, their acceptance.

I thank you for the unlikely people that you have introduced me to. I use this word as I am sure there have been many divine introductions. Isn't that exciting? Different folk! You are teaching me through relationships new things about myself - things that I sometimes don't care to own ...things I need to know.

You have given me friends who encourage by recognising gifts you have given me...help me to listen to them, not brush aside their words with false modesty. May I be gracious!

Dear Jesus, in closing, I thank you and praise you for your excellent provision...friends at all levels, all part of my life and experience... beautiful people!

In gratitude,
Kay

PRAYER - SOLITUDE IS MINE

Solitude is mine,
A prayer of thanks for this moment in time,
When I can be alone and free.
Not one other around do I see.
I feel at one with earth and sky,
My thoughts fly free as the wild birds cry.
I lose myself in what must be,
A foretaste of eternity.

PERSPECTIVE

Lord, give us a world perspective.
We know that we are important as individuals to you
Help us to see that your wonderful plan,
For humankind is universal

GRIEF

Shock, denial -
Then finally acceptance.
The love and compassion
Of caring friends,
People who really listen,
To what we are saying.
Lord, help us each one,
When grief becomes
Our experience.

LETTER TO JESUS - FOR FRIENDS

Dear Jesus

Thank you for friends without whom we could not develop and become the people we are.

Thank you for the freedom they give us to be ourselves - not stifling us but allowing us to grow.

Sometimes even the negative experiences of life, rather than cause an obstacle, create in us a challenge.

You know, Jesus, I was feeling very hurt recently over what I thought was an unfair criticism. I felt so strongly the need to justify myself.

However, when the initial anger subsided, I realised that this was a great opportunity to show your love. I guess, dear Lord, it really was a case of learning to act rather than react.

As we accept each other in friendship, there will be times when these things happen. We just pray that you might help us exercise the great privilege of forgiveness, one to another, so that we may all grow in your love.
Amen.

SNIPPET
An autumn leaf
Falls upon the water.
Our life drifts by.

LOVE

The greatest gift is love.
Thro' all eternity –
Across the sands of time,
The warmth of love will fan the ebbing fire,
'til flames again leap high.
As together by God's Grace,
We find this precious gift
And once again, life face.

Love can conquer all –
It melts the cynic's heart.
It flows out to touch the barren waste
Of lives that fall apart.
It takes away the angry word,
The cruelty of greed,
Awakening in its path, new awareness,
To those in need.
Compassion then becomes a river running wide.
No longer from involvement,
Do we flee –
Or try to hide.

So let us seek to love
Above all desire this gift from God.
For only then – will we walk
In the steps, our Lord has trod.

LOVE - GOD IN YOU

When I love you – I love not only you but God in you.
When I hurt you, not only is it you that feels that hurt –
but God in you.

Perhaps if we considered this more often – we would
find ourselves showing more love to one another.

ACCEPTANCE   June 1982

I marvel, Lord, that you can see
Our life as a tender green shoot.
The seed from which you planted,
In love was given root.

Patiently you walk beside us.
Whether valleys, high or low,
You nurture us so gently –
Until, in time, we grow.

You accept us as we are.
Our potential, you can see.
In love, you help to show us,
The people we can be.

And so, Oh Lord, we pray,
That you might give us grace,
To have this same acceptance,
When in this life with others,
You bring us face to face.

TALKING TO GOD – WHAT MATTERS

Lord, I want to be honest –
About things that really matter in life
Help me to speak as I truly feel.

Not to say what I think –
Is expected from me.
Keep me from making snap judgements.
I want to be fair.
If I'm critical, may it be constructive

I don't want to be dogmatic.
Help me to always remember,
That the other person has a point of view.
Teach me when to be silent,
So that I may never give vent
to angry feelings -
In the heat of the moment.
Above all - temper all that I say,
With all your wisdom and love.
In Jesus' name.

SING TO GOD

Sing to God.
Pray in His name.
Love him forever,
He's always the same.

COMPASSION

Compassion cannot be
Just a thing we feel.
It must result in action,
Before it's something real.

Perhaps the love
God gives us,
We often lock away,
Forgetting that His purpose
Is to use it every day.

To let it overflow
As a river running wide,
That flows in never-ending streams,
Reaching faithful as the tide.

DEPRESSION

Lord – why do I feel so empty?
Help me to sort out –
These negative feelings of mine.
Show those around me that there is
A need for me to work this thing through.
Give them patience with me,
When I'm forever going round in circles,
And the word "depression" becomes reality.
Lord, point me in some direction.
Lead me to people who will
Listen and understand,
So that in time, that small glimmer,
At the end of the tunnel,
Will become a blaze of light.

A WOMAN

In the garden of life
You showed me so fair,
A wonderful picture of what I am there.
Lord, thank you that womanhood,
Brings to our race,
The reasoning of life,
Through your wonderous grace.
We look to your Word
And what do we find?
A procession of women
With ministries fine.
We start with redemption
In the dawn of our day,
And finish with glory,
In a beautiful way.
So let me endeavour
To continue to be
The picture of a woman
You painted for me.

SHARE

We can't go back to experience the past,
So let's look forward to the things that will last.
Happiness and love can always be there,
If we allow ourselves a full life to share.

HENRIETTA

THE TALE OF HENRIETTA

This is a once-upon-a-time tale. All good stories start with once upon a time, especially fairy stories! Although wait, this is not a fairy story; it is a giraffe story - one giraffe in particular. Henrietta! This is her story! Henrietta's saga starts in a faraway land, not Africa, where you may be thinking giraffes should really live. But no! Our beautiful long-necked lady hails from a big city called San Francisco in the United States of America.

She lived in a lovely studio, where she, along with her brothers and sisters and other giraffe friends, were created. There, a very clever sculptor would lovingly fashion each one into the unique creature they would become. Using bronze, he made each one special in his or her own way.

It was there that Henrietta met George, the love of her life. Happily, they lived together with not an inkling of the adventures awaiting them far across the sea in the land called Oz. One day there came to the studio a young woman from this far away land! This is her story also! Many years before this happening, she had become a veterinarian, a doctor who looks after animals. She had established a practice in her local area where she would treat all manner of animals who were feeling poorly. Her name was Merry!

Now on this special day, we could say that the fate of Henrietta and George was sealed. Merry had been sightseeing in the area and came across this antique studio in which these beautiful animals lived. It was love at first sight! Merry knew that she wanted to take the graceful Henrietta and George home with her.

Before long, our two friends set sail. Can you imagine their excitement - little did they know what was ahead for them. After some weeks on the high seas, they reached land, where they were met by a very excited Merry in Brisbane, the city in which they would live. They took up residence in Wilston, standing guard outside the cottage, which was the Vet Practice. Here they lived happily for some years. It was a great place, always something to see. If it wasn't the cars passing by, it was the animals who were in and out in a steady stream.

Sometimes the children would come up and stroke them lovingly. They were never lonely. AND then, one terrible night, disaster struck! They were both dozing off to sleep when somewhere around midnight, a truck drove up and out jumped two ruffians who obviously had evil intent. It seemed it was the beautiful Henrietta that they desired. Setting to work with bolt cutters and all manner of things, they released her from her spot on the footpath and huffing and puffing, finally dragged her into their vehicle. Their dastardly deed done, they spirited her away.

Poor George stood there powerless, unable to move. His Henrietta had been taken right from under his great long neck, and there was nothing he could do. You may think that giraffes don't shed tears. However, the next morning, there was a wet patch on the footpath. George was heartbroken. Everyone was heartbroken! Merry, the vets, the nurses and all who worked in the practice could not believe that such a terrible thing could happen.

A friendly policeman was called in and went to work trying to discover some clues as to whom the culprits may be. Why! Oh! Why would anyone steal a giraffe? What would they do with her? This terrible thought kept creeping into the minds of all. Would they sell Henrietta to melt her down for ready cash! Surely not! No one could be so cruel! Or could they? Some time passed by. George stood on the pavement looking depressed and forlorn! Life without Henrietta was unbearable. If only he could tell what he had seen - he was frustrated.

One day a gentleman was seen to come by and place a posy of flowers on George. He knew how George was feeling.

Merry felt very sad for George, knowing how he missed his mate, and scratched her head, trying to think of a way to help him in his loneliness. Then the thought came to her. Of course. The obvious solution - a "Mail-Order-Bride". So, it was to the internet she went to find a dating site for Giraffes. And after much scrolling and lengthy parading of graceful, long-necked, long-legged beauties, George made his choice!

Daisy, his lovely bride to be! It would be some weeks before she would arrive. However, George was in seventh heaven.

Whilst George is happily anticipating the arrival of his Daisy, there are some dark rumblings. Someone unkind is suggesting that she has run off with an Okapi and is kicking her heels up having fun. As if poor George has not got enough to contend with.

Then this person has suggested that Daisy is not a suitable name for a giraffe; in fact, cows are always called Daisy. Our poor George is becoming depressed once again!

He thinks, why is it that people often seem to not celebrate the happiness of others. In the midst of all this, our friendly policeman enters the story again. He has found Henrietta! Well, sort of! She is in 15 pieces and quite headless! What do we tell George?

Where do you think that she was found? Certainly not kicking her heels up with an Okapi. Tragically her dismembered body was found in a local scrap-metal yard. Her head had been sold to a gentleman, who was probably going to hang it in his home. Poor Henrietta! How humiliating!

Merry lovingly collected Henrietta's broken body taking it back to the surgery to see whether she might be able to resurrect it. Sadly, there is a limit to what animal doctors can do. So, an expert in putting giraffes back together needs to be found.

Meanwhile, the search continued for Henrietta's beautiful head. She does need a head - although we could say a headless giraffe could cause a bit of a stir.

Hooray! The kindly gentleman who purchased the head has come forward and returned it. Henrietta is back with us, albeit in many pieces.

Now George is faced with a dilemma. Henrietta will be repaired, hopefully as beautiful as she always was. And here is mail-order-bride Daisy due to arrive any day. George is formidable, but even he doubts his ability to take on two lovely partners.

Finally, the day came. The beautiful Daisy arrived. George could not believe his eyes; one look and he was in love. Daisy was all he had dreamed about and more! He was eager to nuzzle up to her. That in itself is a rather comical thought - two giraffes nuzzling. However, it is part of our story.

Meanwhile, two kindly local gentlemen who had been following this story, who were in the business of putting things together, although perhaps Henrietta may have been a little challenging, stepped forward and offered to give her new life!

While this was happening, George and Daisy were getting along famously. It would be a little while before he could face the problem his threesome was raising.

Giraffes are very resilient animals, and one and all had confidence in George's ability to solve this little quandary! At last, the day arrived. Henrietta came home, complete with bright pink bandages adorning her joins. She looked so fetching, George felt his heart melting all over again. Even Daisy could not help but feel love for Henrietta. She looked so frail and very appealing in her pink.

Merry placed her in her old spot on the footpath outside the surgery, along with Daisy and George. Many friends came to see her, eager to welcome her home. She was now quite famous. Cars even slowed as they passed by, with many waves from their young occupants.

George had been doing much thinking. He realised what a lucky giraffe he was. It would be quite silly to have to choose one above the other. Rather they would all live harmoniously together. And this is what they did. This is a happy, ever after story!

As I am often inclined to do, I have written the giraffe story in rhyme. Through the years, Brother Russell and I have exchanged our poetry, often adding our own bit of verse to enlarge the storyline. Some of that is included in the following.

MAIL-ORDER BRIDE

Henrietta's not coming home,
She's been gone for Oh! So long!
Poor George his hope diminished,
Is trying to be strong.

Perhaps she's found a younger guy,
And they're kicking up their heels.
It could be they're having fun,
Not caring how George feels.

But George has lost his soul mate,
A lonely life is had.
He fears that forever,
He may be alone and sad!

But wait!
There's hope for George in sight.
Forgotten has been the internet.
Surely it can shed new light!

We googled and scrolled,
And lo! We found a site to fit the bill,
A dating page just for giraffes
With questionnaire to fill.

OUR HEARTS ARE HEAVY

Our hearts are heavy,
Our faces sad,
For news of Henrietta
We have had!

Our beautiful giraffe,
Our graceful, long-necked lady
Has been reduced to pieces,
By someone really shady.

She lies alone,
Her head is missing,
That lovely face,
Just made for kissing.

Who has done this dastardly deed?
The culprit is not found.
No doubt in shame, he's hiding,
Somewhere underground.

Her legs and tail are severed.
She needs a good repair.
Oh, Henrietta, just to look.
Almost too much to bear!

Of fair repute
Our Merry is a vet,
But even she is unable
To perfect that skill as yet.

To replace her parts,
A specialist we will find.
A headless lady she will be,
We won't really mind.

For we know our police,
Will surely save the day.
These trusty folk will find her head
They will lead the fray.

And then our giraffe Doc.
Will work his special magic.
No longer will we sit and mourn,
This act so tragic.

It is all a little delicate for George,
To say the least!
For Daisy, his mail-order-bride,
On soon, his eyes will feast.

Oh! What webs we all do weave,
For George, this is a tangle.
Where will his loyalty be?
With this, he has to wrangle!

HE'S AT IT AGAIN.

He's at it Again.
I wish he'd refrain.
Henrietta has flown
She's not coming home
He's full of insults
With little results
We know she has left
Leaving George bereft
But to challenge her age
All women would rage.
Don't Henrietta mock.

Henrietta's confused
Don't be unkind
Her head she has lost
Where is her mind?

Some scoundrel has scampered,
Away with her head.
Where can it be?
We want to be led.

Her body is scattered,
We hope it will mend,
If her head isn't here,
Her life may end.

Her body is weeping
It feels the pain,
All it wants
Is to be whole again!

She has barely escaped
That awful meltdown.
The cad who took her,
On him, we frown!

Was he pursuing
Some ready cash?
Perhaps it was drugs,
That made him so rash.

Whatever the reason,
It is all bizarre.
Poor George is in limbo.
He frets from afar!

To suggest she's cavorting
With a new beau,
An Okapi at that,
Is to bring her low.

Post Neolithic, she is not.
Her age, we won't guess.
It's rude to enquire.
She won't confess.

Soon we'll unravel
This dastardly deed.
All will end well.
Poems we won't need.

HENRIETTA'S HEAD RETURNS

His neck is arching,
His legs are prancing,
Our George is in Heaven.
He's even dancing!

He's heard the news,
Hip, hip Hooray.
Henrietta has a head.
She's back to stay.

Fragmented she is,
It's a bit of a puzzle.
Restore her we will,
Soon they can nuzzle!

The question now is
How much to tell Daisy!
For soon, she'll arrive.
It's all a bit crazy!

We know she expects
That George is her beau.
Henrietta may find,
She's facing a foe!

FACING A FOE

Giraffes are like people.
This problem is tragic.
Somehow we'll need
Some special magic.

These ladies, I'm sure,
Jealous will be.
A threesome won't work.
That's easy to see.

But wait!
We're jumping the gun.
Henrietta needs mending.
Then there'll be fun!

Her head is so gorgeous.
We pray it will stick,
Otherwise, poor George,
will feel rather sick

His anxiety levels,
Are really quite high!
Since he's known the news
He's been heard to sigh.

You see our Henrietta
Was such a stunner!
'Twas unkindly said,
That she'd done a runner.

We know now, of course,
That this was untrue.
She was, in fact, kidnapped,
To melt into glue.

She has been saved
From a sticky fate.
A sorry way it is,
For George to see his mate!

So for now, this saga
And wonder we'll rest.
Daisy's arrival is soon,
What will be next?

HENRIETTA HAS SURGERY

Feel sorry for our lovely
Henrietta.
She is on the table!
With her kind surgeons
Working their magic,
As only they are able.

Her body parts, they are
Knitting together,
With gentle skill.
Shame on those cruel men,
Who so callously thought,
Our giraffe to kill.

Our girl is full of
Great spirit.
She will deal with this well.
A lesson she'll teach us.
Woe to the Villains,
Her body would sell.

To think that they
Chopped her up,
Removing her head
To make matters worse,
She was treated like trash,
And locked in a shed.

Henrietta now is headless no more.
So, with each stitch,
Put in place,
Her lovely long legs
Will be next.
Her body to grace.

Of course, Daisy,
In residence now,
Henrietta is yet to meet.
George is in luck.
Two beautiful ladies,
Will fall at his feet.

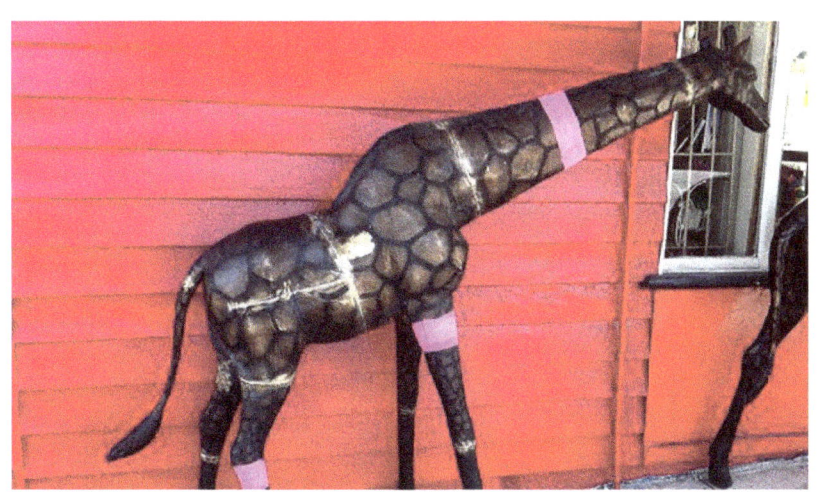

SHE'S BACK

She's back!
Hip hip, hooray.
Our Henrietta
Is here to stay.

She's standing tall
There's quite a crowd
Gathered to greet
Our girl, so proud.

George has a smile
From ear to ear.
He wishes to nuzzle
Or at least get near.

However of course
A dilemma is there.
Daisy is watching,
He must be fair.

Will be some fun
And a bit of a juggle,
To see how George
Will cope with this puzzle.

He had missed Henrietta.
Then along came Daisy.
Full of passion he was,
It's all a bit hazy!

His ladies are both,
Full of charm.
The sidewalk they grace
With amazing calm.

Henrietta has scars
Of a battle well fought.
To be chopped into pieces,
With danger is fraught!

The surgeons with magic
Have repaired the strife.
How grateful we are
They've given her life.

Our two lovelies, it seems,
A friendship have found.
Love there may be,
To stretch all around.

Tales such as this,
We don't leave to chance.
Rather they end
With happy romance!

Our lovely Daisy
Finally, she's here
George, in his excitement
Was seen to shed a tear!

For a while, they can canoodle.
Henrietta's not in sight,
Decision time is looming
George surely will do right,

It is really hard for a giraffe
His relationship to work.
It seems around each corner
A problem there will lurk.

He's already suffered sorrow
When Henrietta disappeared
Now his worry is for Daisy,
Another heartache to be feared!

Meanwhile, his erstwhile love
Is in the surgeon's hand.
George has a migraine,
His head is a tight band!

Like you and I, he's finding
That life can be a maze,
Especially when two loves he has,
Enough to eyebrows raise.
However, George is wise,

And made of sterner stuff.
He knows to bide his time,
Although the going's rough

Perhaps he'll wait
'Til Henrietta, he has seen.
No doubt to hedge his bets,
Will be the way he'll lean!

And so, the saga does not end.
There's still to go some way
True love will surely triumph,
And it will save the day.

GEORGE HAS A DILEMMA

George's head is spinning.
He's been on the booze.
Between Henrietta and Daisy
He'll have to choose.

A headache is his
In more ways than one!
His romances are proving
To be not much fun.

There was Henrietta
His first love, so true.
She disappeared,
He was left to rue.

His grief was helped
By a dating site,
The internet he felt
Would make it right.

When he saw Daisy,
His joy was complete.
In delight, he shook
From his head to his feet.

He had banished Henrietta,
From his active giraffe mind.
After all his Daisy,
Looked to be refined.

Now his loyalty divided
What will he do?
Perhaps he'd take on both,
But could he manage two?

This, of course, is a dilemma,
Not set in stone,
The question is…
Will Henrietta's head come home?

GEORGE IS DISMAYED

George is dismayed,
Daisy is sad.
Somewhere out there
A scurrilous cad!
Is spreading a tale,
Causing Daisy to wail.
He says it's a trick.
Poor George he feels sick,
This lissom lady,
Who is far from shady
His mail-order love
Surely sent from above
Her motives so pure,
He knows she'll endure.
So away with this tale,
These ramblings will fail.
Giraffes are named Daisy.
Tho' some think it crazy.
She uttered a moo,
With their bill and coo!
An endearment, I'm sure.
So rumours, no more.
A cow she is not,
So discard the lot.
Wish them the best,
Give innuendo a rest!

Written by Kay Brothers and sent to Russell Hannah

Russell Hannah replies

I'VE CONSULTED AN EXPERT

I've consulted an expert.
Daisy isn't a cow. And the reason I know
I'll now tell you how.
The expert on Daisys
Lives right here with me.
Daisys all come from Crookwell,
Far away from the sea.
We think that the moo
was heard in the dark,
And it was mistaken,
For a dog's loving bark.
You see every puppy,
That she ever had,
Was always named Daisy,
Both the good and the bad.
She's now writing a book,
When she stops being lazy,
It's all about Puppies,
Called my Crazy, Hazy, Daisys of Summer.

To Russ Hannah from Kay
subject: False Rumours!

GEORGE LOOKS FORLORN

George looks forlorn,
His confidence torn.
That trickster, that cad,
Is making him mad.
He insists Daisy's a pup.
He's making it up!
He says George is blind.
A vet he should find!
Daisy is sad
George is her lad,
He is maligned,
She knows he's defined,
By his charm and his grace,
His handsome face.
To say he is blind,
An insult unkind.
A giraffe cannot sue
Tho' rumour untrue,
They'll stretch their necks high,
There won't be a sigh!
This storm they will weather
At least they're together.
So away with your gall.
Giraffes stand tall!

FALSE RUMOURS Russell Hannah wrote back

I've been worried about George,
For quite some time,
He seems confused,
And not in his prime.
There's a problem he's got,
And it seems to me,
It's not hypertension
And it's not dysentery.
It seems he can't tell,
A giraffe from a pup,
He should see a vet
And get all fixed up.
And I think what the vet
Is certain to find,
That poor old George
Is almost certainly blind.

FINAL FALSE RUMOURS written by Kay

Our George is happy now,
His Daisy, for sure, is not a cow!
A news flash came
To clear her name.
It spoke of dogs that bark,
"Goings on" in the dark.
George had just a little niggle.
However, as he read, there came a giggle.
His Daisy saw the funny side,
They had been taken for a ride!
To say that puppies are all "Daisies,"

They could just as easily be "Maisies."
It is a story tall...
It does not stand but fall!
George and Daisy do not care,
Their love is in the air.
They'll stretch their necks,
And bill and coo!
And nowhere will you hear a moo!

Humour and Fun

STIFF LEGS   March 1981

My legs are stiff,
My back does ache.
A muscle twinges
With each step I take.
I bend and stretch
And touch my toes.
I run on the spot
then bend myself low.
I puff and pant
And roll on the floor.
The family laugh,
And scream for more.
I only hope it's worth the pain,
To once again,
My figure regain.

CRACKLE June 2020

Cousin Rachel has a pet!
It is a pig, would you believe!
She is quite pretty, it is amazing
The compliments she does receive!

I can just imagine as you read,
In your mind, you see this little treasure.
She is very cute, is quite petite
And is loved beyond measure.

I had never heard of a pet pig
And she is quite a little lady
Her intellect is high
She never has been shady.

An apple a day she does enjoy
I guess to keep the vet away,
A belly rub and a bubble bath
Her beauty regime for each day.

She loves to exercise,
To walk the street.
She has her own little coat,
And loves each dog to greet.

She perhaps does know
That she is smarter than they.
However, that bit of knowledge,
She would never convey.

Her name is Crackle,
An apt name, you'll agree.
She is now fully grown
And roams the house free.

So if you are thinking
In a pet to invest,
Please remember our Crackle.
She'll pass every test

WHITE SHEETS

Do you know
what I really like?
Climbing into bed
Twixt fresh white sheets
By Crike!

A wonderful sensation.
I cannot think of when –
I did not feel elation
As I snuggled into them.

OH! THE MYSTERY

A sentinel stands on rickety post,
Clad in old tin,
Soon a sad ghost.
So many old friends lost in the crowd,
Voices now silenced,
Technology bowed.

Our pen we've laid down,
High tech in its place.
Its use has diminished
Tis' farewell to grace.
Today we use e-mails and things of same ilk,
For me, it's comparing old hessian and silk.

A source of mystery just for me,
Always will the post-box be.
With eager hands, I thus explore
Its cavern deep and hope for more.
These days my box is but a slit upon a unit's wall.
It has not lost its magic as the Postie makes his call.

Will it be a letter, perhaps a hasty scrawl,
Or a grand epistle, its reading to enthral?
It may be a card from a place exotic,
Or dare I say it… Something
Quite erotic!

Then, of course there's junk mail.
To this I don't object…there's always something there
That I can re-direct.

Even my better half will welcome it with glee,
For often, it will lead to a happy shopping spree.
I found my cleaning lady from a leaflet in the box.
My husband is in heaven
For she'll even darn his sox.

Then there are birthdays when happy wishes shower.
I like to place them on the shelf
Along with all the flowers.
It's hard to put a fax or an e-mail on the hutch...
They do look rather silly
I don't think we'd bother much.

Who would gather e-mails, and with ribbon
Carefully tie,
To read again across the years,
With joy and tearful sigh.
So when you send a letter, with the wisdom you impart
I'll carefully fold its pages and keep it in my heart.
Tomorrow once again, comfort will I draw,
From its kindly-worded message
And insight there I saw.

Some things are superseded, and this is rightly so.
Let's keep the humble letter.
Please don't let it go!
I'm not a high-tech girl, do listen to my plea.
Help prolong the mystery...
And drop a line to me.

THE TINNY RAMBLE

Dear friends,

You may remember that Russell's big impulse buy last year was a piano which lives in our holiday house in Noosa. Probably the lid has been lifted once, perhaps twice. This year he went one better and came home one day with a little "Tinny". In case you are wondering, No! He is not an avid fisherman; in fact, he does not like fishing as he hates killing fish!

This momentous event happened in early February this year. The boat sat on the trailer in our garage for at least the next four months. Finally, with the help of our friend Rob, they managed to finally get it into the water, through the loch to the jetty at the bottom of our garden. It sat there for the next few months until one weekend, Russell got the urge to take to the water. What a comedy of errors. Firstly, me with my poor old knees and my unsteadiness had a big problem climbing in. Then the engine would not start. We were just about to give up when it finally kicked over, and off we went, managed to get down the river, around the corner a short way, when it gave a splutter and stopped dead...this time it could not be revived.

A kind boatie offered to tow us back to the jetty. He left us in the middle of the river opposite our jetty, with Russell assuring him that we would use our oars and row in. That would have been fine except that when he went to get the oars, he remembered that he had left them in the garage, so he had to use his hands to paddle the boat in. As this was happening, I managed to slip off the seat onto the floor. There was no way I could get up. It took ages for Russell to finally get me on my feet. Getting me out was another difficulty...I could just imagine the spectacle it must have been. I hot-footed it up to the house, determined never to set foot in the boat again.

This was not the end of the story! Russell got back in, refusing to give up. Eventually, the engine kicked over...he raced up and asked me to come, and we would finally get our outing up the river. You can imagine my response! He was back in half an hour, dripping wet (I might add he was wearing shoes and socks, jeans etc. with his mobile phone in his pocket.) Somehow, he had fallen in, the boat had got away from him, and he had to swim out to rescue it. He was so disgusted that he decided that by hook or by crook, he would have his outing downriver, which he did before coming home to tell the sad tale. That little episode cost us $400 for a new phone, and I imagine a bit of loss of face.

May you think that is the end of the tale? Not so! However, you would tire of reading it. ...suffice to say that the boat has still not been used. It sank in our recent deluge of rain, which is another story. Once it was refloated, it then had to be towed back to the public jetty, and where is it now? Sitting once more on its trailer in our garage (motorless), no doubt waiting for the next chapter of its life to begin.

With love,
Kay and Russell

ODE TO THE TINNY

Where has the tinny gone?
Is a common cry,
Where is it hidden
Have you got it high and dry?

My friend, you have hit the nail
On its proverbial head.
We had little choice.
It has left its watery bed.

Instead, it sits on high,
Feeling very sad,
Awaiting someone's loving care,
To restore the fun it had.

Perhaps it feels aggrieved,
Even deserted, no doubt,
At the treatment, rough
That we have meted out.

There was no time
To use kid gloves.
We left in haste,
A way which no one loves.

We hooked it up
And to Brisbane drove.
It now does stand
Part of a treasure trove.

It really is quite pretty,
In leafy green surround
Among chooks and bits and bobs,
It can be found.

There are even a few pussy cats
Who in it like to sleep.
I guess a little demeaning,
When it comes from water deep.

Even we do not know
What its fate will be,
An owner kind would be the go.
It's what we'd like to see!

We want to give our tinny
A chance to really shine.
Someone who would her cherish
Would really do us fine,

It does not like to feel
That it has no self-worth.
It longs to be of use,
And put aside the mirth.

There were many jokes at its expense
And comedy did provide.
Some folk even did respond
With words that were quite snide.

We will now work hard
To see you have much more.
So little tinny we'll do our best
Your future to secure.

I BAKED A CAKE

I baked a cake.
Oh! What a flop.
Would you believe,
They ate the lot?

BACK TO SCHOOL

Back to school,
Oh, what a relief!
The holidays we've weathered,
Without coming to grief.
The house is quiet,
No shouts or strife.
What will we do?
It's all so new!
Just give me a day
Of feeling free
And I'll be ready
The housework to see!

A BIT OF NONSENSE

I once heard a crook
Had stolen a chook.
He wrapped it in foil,
Put it on to boil,
And never again did he look!

The chook boiled dry.
The crook did cry.
Served him right,
He got not a bite.
At least he had a good try.

LITTLE PIGGY   March 1983

Cute little piggy sits on my table.
I guess you're wondering if this is a fable
He's white and green with a flower blue,
It almost looks that it on him grew.
Perhaps you think I'm a silly old fox.
Have you guessed? He's my moneybox!!

A MENTAL ELF

A mental elf,
Sounds just the go
Where will I find him?
Is he on show?

In other words
Is he for sale?
Or for hire, and
I guess he's a male.

Have you ever wondered,
Why goblins and elves
And all of that ilk,
Are different to ourselves.

Mostly they are little men,
Wearing costumes of bright green.
I guess to their surroundings blend
To many, they're unseen.

Not often are little ladies.
Cavorting among the trees
I guess we have the fairies
Not everyone can see.
In the world of magic.
Perhaps that needs to be.

I had a friend who swore
She had fairies in her tree.
I digress, it is the mental elf
Who holds appeal.

He sounds just what I need.
You say he is for real!
Does it mean my inner soul,
My mind and all I am,
Must practise being mindful?
To admit this little man?

Not everyone will find
In him, that self-same strength
Our minds we must prepare
It is a practice of some length

But when we are in tune,
And lifelike, sinking sand
He knows our pain
And takes us by our hand

Because he is a mental elf,
He helps our mind stay strong.
He takes away "the can't do" thoughts,
And shows us when we're wrong.

He leads us to the folk
With whom to walk beside.
No man is an island,
It takes help to turn the tide!

That you need to ask for help,
Do not feel false guilt.
There's strength in reaching out,
It's how relationship is built.

So, I think I know
Where that mental elf resides
I'll take him on board
Together we will ride.

Do not reach for him
Then put him on the shelf.
He needs to be in constant use
He's there to help yourself.

If you cannot find him
Please ask you'll find his guise.
They will know just where to look.
Just choose a friend who's wise!

This is the end to this ode,
A postscript, I would add.
I would love to see a female elf,
Her input would be fab!

REFLECTION ON JENNY JOSEPH'S POEM   2013

I am the age! I now can wear the purple and the red.
I can read that poem with gusto and laugh to hear it read.

I can be a tad eccentric; some might call it odd,
For now, a different path I walk, my feet with fun are shod.

I now have the wisdom gleaned from learning just "to be".
Satisfaction comes when it's OK to just be me.

So thank you, Jenny Joseph, for showing me the way.
The seeds of wisdom you have sown will help me join the fray.

I may not gobble sausages, or even learn to spit,
However, other little foibles will help me do my bit.

With friends, I'll share one coffee and talk for hours on end
Our laughter and our banter will help our spirits mend

We'll dress to please ourselves and be a mite extreme.
Our families look in wonder, just hoping it's a dream.

In youthful years we have had our share of being proper,
A bit afraid to take a risk in case we come a cropper.

I write this little Ode to those who fit the bill.
There's a long way yet to go before we're over the hill.

JUMPING CASTLES

I've decided that you
Don't have to be a certain age
Or even a child
Come on. The world is our stage.

Let's jump on the castle,
Let down our hair.
Shed our inhibitions
'tis the fun of the fair.

We'll leap and laugh
In pure delight,
The wind in our hair
Perhaps we're a sight.

Who cares how we look,
For a moment in time.
Please don't disturb,
We're waiting in line.

Our friends think we're crazy
And maybe we are.
You may even join us.
Come be a star!

Forget the stiff legs,
The aches and the pain.
We'll give it a go,
Who knows what we'll gain?

Even now I can hear
The sceptics out there,
They think we're eccentric
Tho' little we care

So nice it is
To break the mould
Of those who dictate
When one is old!

OH! WHAT FUN

Oh! What fun,
To sit in the sun.
In the warmth
Of its rays,
I find solace for days.

A GROUP OF LIMERICKS!

To write limericks all the time
For someone like you is fine.
Oft I can't find a word to rhyme.
I'm almost stuck as I write this line.
Is it of something sinister, a sign?

*

Could you help me find
Where I've put my mind?
If you know, do not be unkind.
Has it been sidelined,
Because I slipped on an orange rind?

*

A duck one day met a turtle,
Dressed she was in becoming purple.
She introduced herself as Myrtle
With dainty pink spots on her kirtle.
Into a romance they did hurtle!

*

The cup said to the mug,
Please give me a hug.
No, said mug, let's cut a rug.
Along came a thug,
And gave them a slug.

They never got to dance,
Nor even did they prance.
The thug was eaten
By some ants.
They hugged while they had a chance.
Truly it was a wise stance!

CREATED NOT MADE!

Writers! Created, not made.
Do please discuss with me,
If I practice really hard,
Will I a poet be?

Will I read Thesaurus,
Until my eyes turn red,
And then with "gay abandon"
See where my thoughts are led?

Should I brush up on my Shakespeare
And others of same "ilk"?
I'll try digesting meat,
And say goodbye to milk.

I'll remember "catchy phrases"
That can be somehow put to use.
I'll write them in my notebook,
And sit for hours and muse.

For if indeed a writer's made
From working really hard,
Then perhaps one day
I too will also be a bard.

However, I've a feeling
Created I should be
With inspiration great
For all the world to see.

Oh! Never mind it was a thought
Tossed from me to you.
Think about it now
And tell me how you grew.

Kay with husband Russell at her 80th party.

CELEBRATIONS

ODE To KAY on her 80th Written by her brother Russell

When you wake up in the morning and you throw
the blankets back,
And when you stand and straighten up, the bones begin to crack,
And your muscles shriek in protest as you hobble from the bed,
And the bathroom mirror tells you things you'd rather
were not said,
And like a vintage car, you must warm up before you go,
You've reached the way of life for those who've made
the big Eight 0!

And if people say behind your back,
There's one of those old dears,
And all the studs you used to know, have now turned into steers,
And if you like a glass of water, more than glasses of fine wine,
Then I guess at last you've made it, you've crossed the eighty line.
But even when you're eighty, there's plenty left to do,
For it's the ideal time to make "a whole of life" review,
You can do some navel-gazing and reflect upon the way,
From birth, your life has progressed to where you are today. Born
in 1940 with the country in the wars,
You carefully selected the best progenitors,
For a mother and a father, you got Beattie, you got Lyall,
Who made growing up a pleasure, and not an awful trial.

You were a perfect daughter, at least to be one you did try.
But you wouldn't eat your kidneys in the steak and kidney pie,
You'd never touch that lambs fry or pick the bones from fish,
And never would you eat that tripe - your mother's favourite dish.

You grew up in the shire, went to Miranda School,
Spent times at all the beaches and in the swimming pool,
You went to High School at Jannali; the school's first captain
You became,
Then went to work for Qantas, shorthand typing was your game.

You came back to the shire, you'd developed people skills,
Worked in the doctor's surgery, helping people deal with ills.
Your life was on a straightforward path, at least that's
what it seemed,
Until fate by name of Russell stepped in and intervened.

You knew that fellow Russell - he always hung about,
Night and day, he'd pester you and want to take you out,
He wouldn't go, he wouldn't stop, so in the end you said,
If you cannot beat 'em, join 'em, so the two of you got wed.

And now you're married 60 years, he really is quite tame.
And he really is quite useful, and you've had someone to blame.
You moved up to the Sunshine State, where
the climate is conducive,
To raising kids in families that are always quite inclusive.

The babies came along of course, four before a pause,
You may have had a couple more except you learned the cause.
So you raised them up to adults, and really in the main,
You seemed to be successful, for all look fairly sane.

When they spread themselves around the world
and left the family nest.
You heaved a heavy sigh - at last, you'd earned some rest.
You took rest time up in Noosa away from Brisbane's bustle,
Worked for the church and charities and spent lots of time
with Russell.

But the kids came back as kids will do, and when they did
they brought
A little Angelina, your very first granddaughter.
Now when your girls saw this, they thought they'd like a bub,
So off they went and quickly joined - the famous puddin' club.
Now she's got some hordes of them. There's Chloe, Bekkah, Jake
There's Isaac, Bella, Sasha, Jude. The next ones will be 'Great',
And as you've now reached eighty and your life songs still is
sung,
You've proved that old adage wrong, that only the good die
young.

Russell Hannah: March 2020.

MY BIRTHDAY   March 2006

My birthday is a special day.
At least that's what the greetings say.
What if you are old and grey?
Far better if you're young and fey.

I'm 66, clickety-click.
Will bingo be my next new kick?
Is it time the years to tick,
Is life about to play a trick?

Perhaps now time to be unique.
Go abroad and find a Greek.
For that, I am a little meek,
But new horizons I will seek.

I'll wear the purple 'tis the time.
Be eccentric; it's not a crime.
Friends will cry, you're fine, just fine,
At 66, who walks the line?

MY BIRTHDAY   March 2007

When birthdays come around,
We celebrate anew
And it becomes a custom
To pen a line or two.

Last year was all so easy,
For it was 66.
The words just tumbled out,
A great eclectic mix.

It may be trite, albeit true.
I'm closer now to Heaven,
For when tomorrow dawns
I'll say "hello" 67.

Something is on my mind.
It is that old word leaven.
Not many words are found to rhyme,
With this rogue 67.

Leaven, the agent that makes the dough to rise,
Transforming the loaf with its surprise.
So may this birthday be a rising of courage, not fear,
As I look to celebrating another birthday year.

DANCE AND SING

Let us laugh and dance and sing,
Showering each other
With the joy
That God's love can bring.

HEAD IN SHAME

Lord – I hang my head in shame
for losing sight of you,
Who came to man, a gift of love,
To make our lives anew.
And so, to you this Christmas,
My gift of love I bring.
Take my all, it is your own,
My Father, Lord and King.

BAPTISM

Today is a happy day
The day that the Lord has made
the day of your Baptism.

The day that you chose,
To respond to God's call
On your life.

A day of promise,
of commitment,
a precious day of blessing.
God and you.

A day of celebration,
of thanksgiving
as you take your place
in the great family of God.

A day of joy
as along with you,
we reaffirm our vows
Made long ago.

This day is beautiful,
a day of grace.
We are filled anew,
With the Spirit of God.

Let us praise Him.
Alleluia!

PENTECOST SUNDAY   May 1982

You came as the Dove of Peace.
Your gentle Spirit joins with mine.
The love we feel together,
Surely is the sign.

How can mere words express,
The joy I really feel?
Dear Lord, I thank and praise you.
On me, you've set your seal.

A promise at the beauty,
Of life that's yet to come,
That day of true fulfilment,
When Lord, we'll all be one.

JOY TO YOUR WORLD

Joy to your world at Christmas,
A time of peace and love.
As the blessing of the Christ Child,
falls down from God above.
A time of great rejoicing,
As we praise our Lord and King.
Lift high our hearts and voices,
As to Him, our worship bring.

PENTECOST

It's your birthday, it's your birthday,
All have a happy day.
Church, lift your voice in praise,
We'll come together and pray.

This is a joyous time,
We'll light the candle of love,
This day so long ago,
God gave this gift from above.

A gift so special,
It sets all hearts aflame.
It fills us all with a boldness,
Jesus, your name proclaim.

Happy birthday, dear church,
Please unwrap your gift.
Don't let it go unnoticed,
This will our spirits lift.

Go back across the years,
That upper room recall
So brightly burnt the flame.
It holds us in its thrall.

God gave His Holy Spirit
A down payment for each one.
He's blessed us without measure,
With promise of life to come.

Let's celebrate this day,
With a smile upon our face.
Clap our hands and dance.
This is a day of grace.

REFLECTIONS ON CHRISTMAS!

The Christ Child is among us!
We welcome Him with love.
The refugee looks for Him.

Where are you, Lord?
Is his plea, while we stand,
Lives full to the brim

Yes, Lord, your mum and dad.
Refugees also looking for a warm place
to give birth

A stable. It was simple and bare
And there you lay,
the King of all the earth.

At times we talk
Of entertaining Angels unaware.
This was more, so much more!

I wonder did that innkeeper
Ever know the import of that night?
Of those special things he saw.

Today we have those who also flee,
Who from torture and terror,
Become the needy and the lost.

We need to welcome them,
And help them find their place.
We may all have to count the cost.

Help us to open eyes and hearts
That may have closed.
May we have compassion for this day.

What are your thoughts Lord, when among us,
You are walking? Have you a broken heart,
For your people in this fray?

This Christmas, as we celebrate
Let our birthday gift to you.
Be a grateful heart.

A heart where gratitude is expressed
In love and solidarity for the hurting,
May we play our part!

ON THE O BIRTHDAY   July 1996

We'll sing and dance.
And shout hurrah.
Again, we'll recall our
Youth afar.
How many O's do we have left?
I fear they are dwindling, becoming bereft.
No time to ponder this issue sore,
I'm just believing there'll be many more.

CHRISTMAS   2005

Poor Santa has a problem,
He's eaten far too well.
His ribs have turned to lolly sticks.
A habit he must quell.

His tiny clients have bribed him,
As they sat upon his knee.
Santa loves his special treats,
It's plain for all to see.

The Doc is very stern,
As he looks upon his chest.
Ho, Ho, Ho says Santa,
The Doc is not impressed.

You'll never make another year,
Of Santa-ring, he said.
You cannot keep indulging.
I'm ordering you to bed.

Away from all these lollies,
All these sticky little mites,
You'll be a healthy Santa.
Just forgo those little bites.

But rest, and your ribs will mend.
They will be as good as new.
Just try a glass of beer a day,
And you will be "true blue."

ANNIVERSARY RAMBLE   2021

On the 4th of February, Russell and I will have chalked up 60 years of marriage. Even as I write this, I am even finding it an incredible milestone and am wondering how those 60years could have vanished the way they have. It is as if they have sprouted wings and flown away.

Of course, 60 years cannot disappear without many experiences, both happy and sad, remembering as I have often written that sorrow and joy are sisters who live in the same house. To be totally honest, it is not the easiest thing to do to live with the same person for that length of time and not give way to frustration and lots of other little niggles. Sometimes we have to keep our tongues which can be sharp and cutting, from giving each other a strong serve. At times we need the patience of Job and the forgiveness that is the cornerstone of our faith.

As I look back over those years, I give thanks for the great friendships which we have had and the importance of their support. Many of those years were spent in other places without the benefit of family presence. To all our friends, we say a big thank you for your listening ears and wise counsel. It was and is still invaluable.

Alison and Kay enjoyed the "Van Gogh" digital spectacular experience.

Meeting with Kangaroo Point Neighbourhood Watch

COMMUNION.   July 1982

Lord –
This morning it was communion,
Your supper – your wonderful meal of celebration,
The time when we all gather together
To remember you – to feast with you
And the whole body of Saints past and present.

I'm sure, Lord, you meant this to be
A really joyous occasion,
A time of harmonious fellowship
With you and one another.

Lord, what a lot of long, serious faces.
Please forgive me if I'm being irreverent,
But – where is this wonderful joy we're always talking about?
Is it wrong to want the reality of that?
And surely in your great sacramental meal, we should be
showing it.

Enthuse our hearts,
Let your love shine through
So that our faces can't help but reflect that wonderful joy –
Lord, start with me.

Amen.

CHRISTMAS   1980

Joy to your world at Christmas.
A time of peace and love.
As the beginning of the Christ child
Falls down from God above.
A time of great rejoicing,
As we praise our Lord and King.
Leap high our hearts and voices
As to Him, our worship bring.

CELEBRATION   July 1982

Dear Jesus
Yesterday my friend's son was 21,
Her mother was 80 –
And what a wonderful celebration we had.

Thank you for times like this,
Times of gathering together,
Happy families, close friends
And the joy that they bring.

Thank you that in this world
Where so much unhappiness reigns
That we can come together and
Demonstrate your love.

Perhaps in a small way, on occasions such as these, we can't help but catch a glimpse of the relationship you intended for your church here on earth.
Amen.

CALYPSO SONG

Chorus   Come one, come all, let us rejoice,
              In glad praise with heart and voice.
              Welcome Christ, this happy morn
              Hallelujah, our King, is born.

V1. Long, long ago, in a far-away land
        Wise men travelled the desert sand.
        They came a tiny babe to greet
        To lay their treasures at his feet.

V

V2. In the heavens high a bright star shone
        As shepherds knelt in joyful song
        Carols echoed through the night.
        Angels arrayed in garments of light.

V3. Worship Him – our God above.
        Thank you, Jesus for your grace and love.
        Knock upon the Heavenly door.
        It is open for evermore.

V4 So, join your Spirit, everyone,
       In one accord, our Saviour come.
       Christmas bells ring loud and clear,
       Alleluia salvation is here.

V5. So join your Spirit everyone
        In one accord our Saviour come
        Christmas bells ring loud and clear
        Alleluia salvation is here.

V6. I can't lend you love –
So please don't ask.
Each of us can find it
It's a very pleasant task.

V7. Open yourself to all around
Wherever you may be
And soon you'll find a warm response –
And happiness you'll see.

V8. For it seems to steal upon you
Just like a gentle dove.
And then you'll know the fullness
Of a life that's filled with love.

GOOD FRIDAY

I sit in quietness at your feet
And worship silently.
I feel your anguish hanging there
As you pay the price for me.

EASTER DAY

I come in joyous praise
On this happy Easter morn.
My heart sings Alleluia
For a life that's been reborn.

ADVENT 2015

Good morning, dear friends, we are now in the lovely season of Advent, tomorrow being the first Sunday. A time when we celebrate the first coming of Christ and look forward with hope and anticipation to His promised Second coming.

Many churches (our previous church among them), have the lovely liturgy of lighting the advent candles. The four candles are on a Christmas wreath; one is lit each Sunday up until Christmas, the fifth and centre candle represents Jesus and his coming into our world. So, we light the candle of hope, of peace, of joy, and love. The fifth candle is the Christ candle which is lit on Christmas Eve.

This is lit with the prayer that Jesus will be born in us anew, in our hearts, our minds, our lives, that the light of His life shine in us and lead us to the truth of God with us, God for us, and God in us!

Come, Jesus, Come!

EASTER 1987

We praise you, Lord
For your gift of love.
We open our hearts and believe.
The warmth of your presence eternally there
Holy Spirit, your gift we receive.

MY 7th BIRTHDAY

It is strange how certain events never leave you. One would not think that a seventh birthday would be a momentous occasion! Perhaps it is remembered because it is the only birthday party as a child that I can recall having.

We lived in those days at the beach, not only at the beach, however right on the beach, a short little track and then the dunes, then miles of uninhabited coastline. We were one of not more than half a dozen houses on that little stretch of bushy forest.

To my childish mind, our house was really something; however, seen through my adult eyes, it was probably pretty basic. Built of timber and painted quite an uninteresting brown, it stood not in a garden, however surrounded by Pandanus palms and natural beachy flora. The soil, of course, was mainly sand, which did not equate with successful gardening.

I loved the fact that it was upstairs and downstairs. Although having said that, it was rather an odd configuration. One would enter into the kitchen, which with the bathroom shared the bottom level. The very wide staircase rose out of the kitchen and entered the upstairs level on a very wide verandah, which was closed in with windows all along facing out to sea. Behind the staircase on this level was the lounge room, with a bedroom on either side and another room which my mother used as a sewing room, which you would enter from the verandah. I still have memories of all those windows having blackout blinds in the early forties during the second world war. There was an old wireless in a cabinet in the lounge. It was our entertainment. I can still see myself sitting on the floor, ears glued listening to 'Dad and Dave', and the 'Picture of Dorian Grey.'

My party was held outside. This was the day of party hats. I can still see my mother making them for the eight little girls, with lots of crepe paper and multicoloured frills; quite stylish they were. The young guests arrived wearing their Sunday best, pretty little dresses, shiny shoes and short white socks. We had lots of games, popular at that time. Could you imagine the seven-year-olds of today playing "Drop the Hankie?" Things were much more unsophisticated in the 40s. In fact, I can remember going to parties, and my mother, or grandmother with whom I had lived for a year, giving me a coin wrapped in the comer of a pretty new handkerchief as a gift for the party girl. When I see the parties that our grandchildren and their friends have today, it is certainly a far cry from yesteryear!

To this day, almost seventy years later, I still recall the names of some of my little friends, although as we moved just a couple of years later to the city, I was never to see them again.

I will always remember Beverley. She had injured her foot badly a day or so prior to the party. I can still see her sitting on the running board of the old ute with her leg up to this day. I can still experience the sad feeling I had for her! I kept looking at her, feeling sorry and trying to think of ways to include her in the fun. Perhaps this was my introduction to compassion. It is the earliest experience to which I can relate that feeling. Is that I wonder why this really insignificant event stays with me. I have always felt compassion for people in trying times. Somehow, I think our world today needs a good dose of it

Perhaps you feel the same?
This is just a little sharing from my past.... random thoughts. It seems that as we grow older, nostalgia is often our companion in life.
Kay

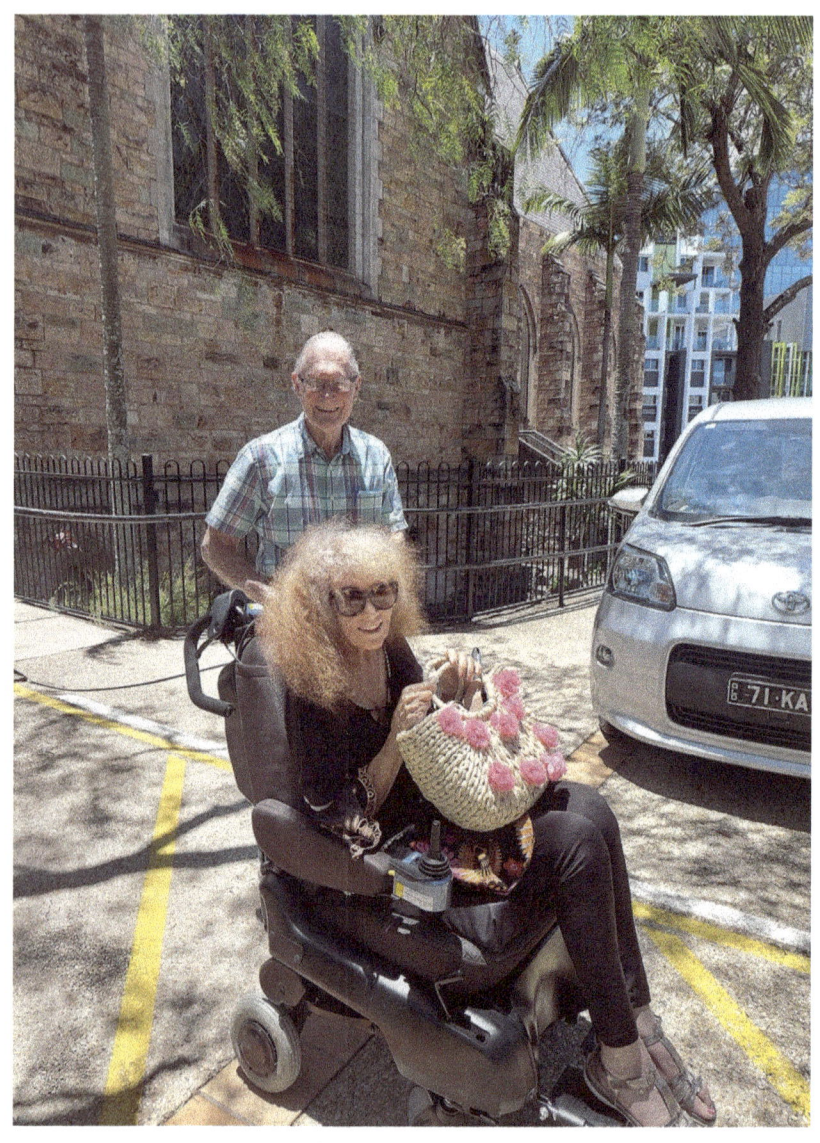

Here we are arriving at church in the new Toyota built especially for this wheelchair. It has liberated our movements around Brisbane.

CHRISTMAS 2021

Dear Friends,
This comes to send you a happy, blessed Christmas greeting in 2021.

This year has been somewhat challenging. The year began with a nice celebration of our 60th wedding anniversary at the Story Bridge Hotel with our family. From then on, things went haywire! I had a few falls in April and ended up having a brain bleed which saw me in a coma for two weeks, followed by surgery and a 14 week-long stay in hospital and rehab. Sadly, this has greatly affected my mobility, and I need to use a wheelchair. I came home at the end of July and have now spent about five months at home with Russell as my primary carer. For the first 12 weeks, we were provided with a Transition Care Program with some lovely ladies who came every morning to help with showers and changing. Since then, we have continued with assistance from a group named Angels in Aprons, who are coming on weekdays to give some help as needed. The kids also come a few days a week and at weekends and make many meals for the freezer too!

We have enjoyed many visits, cups of tea and lunches with friends and family since returning home, however, we were unable to leave the unit until about a month ago when we purchased a small Toyota Porte, which has an electric wheelchair as the front passenger seat. This has been exciting! We have been able to return to going to church on Sundays and meet with our Neighbourhood Watch friends at our weekly coffee mornings. We can also go out for coffee or wherever we need to go, which has really given us some much-missed freedom. My lack of voice because of Parkinson's continues to be very challenging; however, I try to make the most of it whenever I do have a little volume.

All the kids and grandkids are well and still close by, except for Andrew in Hong Kong, whom we hope will be able to visit early next year, depending on the COVID situation.

Life is not as easy as it once was…I am grateful for those who encourage me and give me hope - lots of good friends, thank you all…You are loved and appreciated!

I would like to share that little verse of Michael Leunig's… it is pertinent for me, perhaps you also?

HOW TO GET THERE
Go to the end of the path,
Until you get to the gate.
Go through the gate and head
straight out towards the horizon.
Keep going towards the horizon.
Sit down and have a rest every now and then.
But keep on going, just keep on with it.
Keep on going as far as you can.
That's how you get there!

We wish you all peace and joy as you celebrate this happy season. May our God who sent his Son into our world at this special time help us all in this coming year to become a rainbow in someone's dark cloud.

Christmas blessings and love to all.

Kay and Russell xxxxx

Christmas with all our grandchildren.

Alison, Kay, Russell, Merry and David

www.ingramcontent.com/pod-product-compliance
Lightning Source LLC
Chambersburg PA
CBHW042129160426
43198CB00022B/2956